Dedication
Life is full of opportunities!
This book is dedicated to those special people who find the
courage to reach out for theirs and to all the people who
have helped me paint the canvas of my life.

Published in 2001 by
Biznet Publishing Company Inc.
6541 Lisgar Dr.
Mississauga Ontario Canada
L5N 7P6
biznet@techcomnet.com

Canadian Cataloguing in Publications Data

West, Douglas Warren, 1946 –
Inside Out

ISBN   09683931-3-6

First Printing May 2001
1. Sales 2. Business

Editor: Leona Baldwin
Graphic Design and Cover: Brian Naidu
Page Layout: Brian Naidu

Printed and Bound in Canada

About the Author

Doug West is a successful business book author. 'Inside Out' is his third book following his best seller on the fundamentals of customer first selling presentations entitled 'Professional Selling Secrets' and his current best seller on the entrepreneurial experience 'It's Your Frog …Warts And All'. He is  also one of North America's premier business speakers on the topics of sales motivation and the power of entrepreneurship. He writes and speaks from extensive experience having been a successful salesperson and sales director for over twenty-years. Since leaving a senior management position in the corporate sector over ten years ago, he has enjoyed a lively and productive career running his own company specializing in developing training seminars for a diverse clientele. In addition he began his own publishing company Biznet to handle the distribution and marketing of his books. Doug speaks at over 100 meetings, events and conferences every year.

Foreword

The world of professional sales is not for the weak willed or faint of heart. It tests the courage and commitment of all who take on the challenge of becoming part of it. In most instances sales practitioners must have the drive and determination to create their own opportunities and possess the degree of skills needed to convert them into revenue generating sales. Selling skills however are not in and of themselves the sole criteria needed to face up to and stare down the ongoing challenges they confront. The fact of the matter is, unless salespeople can bring the full weight of their skills and their performance qualities to bear on those challenges they are unlikely to achieve the level of performance they strive for. Today, there is little doubt that top sales professionals apply performance qualities that are equal to or surpass the qualities of the service of product they sell. It's called 'selling from the inside out'.

When I sat down to write this book it was not my intention to put together a 'how to' book on the intricacies of making a sale. Rather, the intention was to increase the readers awareness of the impact performance qualities like positive thinking, self-confidence, self-concept and personal values can have on your effectiveness when applying your selling skills. My purpose is to help you discover and understand more fully the traits and characteristics you can use to keep a positive balance in your professional and personal life.

I have been associated with salespeople in one way shape or form for most of my life. I've been one, managed others and observed even more. Professional salespeople are the heartbeat of every organization that brings a product or service to market. They are the often under-appreciated front line troops in the battle for increased market share and sales revenue. I would like to thank all of the salespeople I've worked with, competed with and swapped war stories with, you have enriched my life. I hope you will find equal measures of information and inspiration in the pages of this book.

Douglas West

INTRODUCTION

*The only thing holding you back from doing
what you can is thinking that you can't.*

The objective of this book is to help you find ways to improve your selling results by combining the selling skills you have with the performance qualities you need. It's your performance qualities that can give you the edge you need in any selling situation. Applying what you learn from this book will help you sustain a higher level of productivity over a longer period of time. The practical insights and ideas found here will help you achieve your professional and personal goals by encouraging you to raise your expectations and personal performance standards.

The ever-changing dynamics of the workplace has created a situation where unprecedented numbers of people are choosing to or being forced to, re-invent themselves and follow new career paths. You may not be doing what you were educated for or trained to do at the beginning of your working life. A lot of people are finding themselves in second or third careers. For a lot of them all or part of their income will be driven by their ability to make sales. Many who find themselves in these new sales driven careers are challenged because of lack of prior experience.

If you number yourself among these people, your future success won't be driven exclusively by your product knowledge or recently acquired selling skills. Your success in facing life in the selling lane will be determined to a large extent by your understanding of how to bring your performance qualities into play. If you are employed as a salesperson by a large organization you will in all likelihood participate in some company sponsored training before you are turned loose on your own. You will be taught what it takes to get in front of customers, uncover their needs and match your line of products or services to those needs. That process involves learning and applying practical and proven sales skills. Even with top-notch training however, you will not be able to get the most out of your expertise and ability until you learn to appreciate the value and benefits of using your performance qualities to sell from the inside out.

Nothing happens until somebody sells something to someone. If you're a new salesperson starting your career and that thought scares you, you're not alone. The fact of the matter is, more people are involved in selling something to someone than any other single job sector in our economy and yet a lot of them would rather do something other than sell, and be something other than a salesperson. For a lot of people the part of selling that overwhelms them is the fear of rejection. The big R word has been responsible for more people deciding on a career change from salesperson to anything as long as selling isn't a part of it, than any other word in the English language. For others it's the fear of failure that haunts them. Unlike a lot of other jobs where the result of daily activities is hard to measure, in the world of professional sales, it's pretty easy to quantify the results of your sales efforts. You either make the sale or you don't.

In most organizations you are part of a sales team. Along with the challenge of competing with competitors there is always the friendly competition among colleagues and team-mates. Everyone is working to reach both individual and team goals. You can always check the standings to see how you and your team are doing. Your sales results indicate where you stand. It doesn't take a degree in rocket science to know your sales are either where they should be, or above or below your expectations. You have the freedom to work harder and learn to work smarter to improve your sales or (sales managers please put the book down) take some down time to enjoy the fruits of your labors. The life of a salesperson can be challenging and tough. It's never dull, but if you wanted dull you should have gone into accounting.

One characteristic common to successful sales professionals is the ability to juggle time and priorities. They are expert at keeping more than one ball in the air at the same time. We all know people who are brilliant linear-minded thinkers. Task oriented people who when they have a job to do are as focused as a bulldog chewing on a bone. Nothing is allowed to interfere with the task at hand. The rigid discipline these people exhibit would make a monastic monk envious. Salespeople need to have a disciplined work ethic in fact they need it more than most people in most other jobs. In order to be successful however, they also need to temper it with flexibility. Professional salespeople have to develop a unique ability to maintain a disciplined work ethic while working through an often-chaotic turn on a dime schedule. They need to be able to move forward and work with a schedule without becoming a slave to it.

They are charged with many responsibilities. In addition to being accountable for generating sales most are directly accountable for managing a sales territory. This can mean anything from keeping call records up to date to budgeting and trouble-shooting. All of which eats into precious prospecting and selling time. Today while it seems like our working days gets longer the time we have to spend gets shorter. Salespeople more so than most, have to learn to spend time resources wisely. Most salespeople find the personal freedom to come and go and work outside the restraints of an office is a double-edged sword.

On one hand you have personal freedom to manage your time. On the other you are personally responsible to make the most of the time you manage. The most productive way to do it is to stay focused on the big-picture! Spend as much time dealing with the have to do's as the like to do's. Work in the moment, with more effort devoted to the here and now. Don't get distracted by insignificant time wasting minutia, like putting out brush fires while the barn burns down. Don't let yourself be easily distracted from your priority activities. Set deadlines and develop timelines for longer-term projects. Work toward a combination of interim and long-term goals and objectives. Work toward your major objectives the same way you would eat an elephant; one bite at a time. Don't hesitate to yell loudly for help when you need it. For everyday low payoff activities, allot some time, get done what you can during the allotted time and move on. Finally make sure you occasionally steal a little 'me time' out of your schedule as a reward for just being you.

We Live and Learn

When we live with an open mind,
we learn to admire what is different.
When we live with competition,
we learn to appreciate winning.
When we live with positive recognition,
we learn to take constructive actions.
When we live with clear goals,
we learn how to stay focused.
When we live with values,
we learn to inspire others.
When we live with a sense of humor,
we learn to enjoy.
When we live with self-worth,
we learn to value ourselves.
When we live with self-confidence,
we learn to admire others.
When we live with humility
we learn how to share the spotlight.
When we live with imagination,
we learn there are no limits.
When we live with determination,
we learn to overcome.
When we live with love,
we learn to be free.

Douglas West

CHAPTER ONE
The Impact of Performance Qualities

Today, the qualities of the salesperson must be equal to or surpass the quality of the product or service being sold.

Every field of endeavor requires an above average output of effort to generate above average results. One of the common denominators found in successful people is the simple fact that they know what their performance qualities are and how and when to use them to get a maximum return on the effort they invest. We know for instance that at every level of performance a few always outdistance the many. There are many capable athletes but few superstars. There are in every field many perfectly adequate people filling their jobs with adequate effort and generating adequate results. We also know that there are a few outstanding performers in every field, professional selling is no exception.

There are certain common characteristics we often attribute to and associate with those around us who we consider to be top performers in their chosen field. Drive to succeed, dedication to excellence and perseverance in the face of challenge to name only a few. I believe people who reach the pinnacle of success are guided by positive emotional and spiritual influences. They resist the temptation to alter their personal values to suit expedient times and places. They have a vision of a better tomorrow and they work hard to put themselves into situations that will create opportunities to move toward their vision. They use a performance quality like self–leadership, to set their own higher than average goals and objectives and then they apply their own demanding performance standards to reach them. They know the importance of continuously building their self-confidence through self-directed positive reinforcement of who they are, what they do and how they do it. They take the time and make the effort to consistently add to the know ledge they have, refine the skills they use and protect the attitude they need. They are the ones who run toward change while others are busy fleeing from it. They combine the previously outlined attributes with some common sense smarts which are used to work out logical and workable solutions to problems they encounter. They finish it off with the energy and dedication needed to do what has to be done when it needs doing. These consistent winners weave all of these and other traits and characteristics into positive performance qualities that form the foundation of satisfying and successful lives and careers.

Here's a question you might want to consider. Do successful people feel better about themselves because of the positive outcomes they produce, or do they produce more positive outcomes because of the way they feel about themselves? The answer is, before you can hope to attain better than average results from what you do, you have to find ways to feel better about the person you are. To reach your peak performance level you need to feel good about yourself physically, emotionally, mentally and spiritually. Your performance qualities can be used as catalysts to bring everything together and help you focus clearly on what needs to be done and how you are going to get it done.

The quality of your daily performance is influenced by both positive and negative factors you encounter. The level of your performance will be a reflection of how successful you are in letting in the positives and keeping out the negatives. When the negatives attacking you are successful in breaching your defenses you are bound to fall under their spell and influence. This results in non-productive 'why days'. These are the days we all have when most of our time is spent asking 'why me'? Why, am I doing this? Why, don't they leave me alone? Why, didn't I take my Mothers advice, and other why-isms brought on by negative thoughts and reflections.

On the other hand when you are firing on all cylinders and your performance qualities are being driven by positive feelings and emotions you experience and participate in more 'my days'. Those are the days you start the day feeling like it's yours. The day belongs to you and you are going to make the most of it. How well you manage your performance qualities directly controls the way you feel about yourself and the actions you take because of those feelings.

Each of us I'm sure has had at least the occasional day when we find it difficult to think clearly, or focus our attention on the subject at hand because we're upset at something we've done or had done to us. The anger and anxiety that results from our inability to 'get over it' and 'get on with it' often keeps us from relaxing and increases an already high level of stress. No one can perform at high levels of effectiveness under those conditions. Knowing how and when to summon the appropriate performance quality to counteract the effects of stress can lessen the number of those performance-draining days you find yourself facing. Using your performance qualities in the right way at the right time will enable you to put yourself in a position more often to meet the challenges you face head on with the full force of the best you have to offer. The relationship between the outcome of your daily performance and the level of your performance qualities works like this:

- The outcome of what you try to do and what you get done is directly influenced and controlled by how you feel about yourself. When you feel positive your performance improves.
- When you bring the full weight of your performance qualities to bear on a challenge the result is more likely to be positive and productive.
- To consistently overcome negative situations, circumstances and challenges you must develop and maintain an effective level of performance quality.

Knowing how to put your performance qualities to work for you can help you take the critical career step up from what you are capable of accomplishing to what you actually accomplish. Trying to perform at an above average level without the use of every tool in your arsenal is physically, emotionally and mentally tiring. You expend vast amounts of energy compensating for the strengths you lack instead of focusing that energy on improving the strengths you have. The effort is there but the factors that determine the outcome of the effort are missing. It's like trying to get a seed to grow in frozen soil. Nothing happens if the soil remains frozen. The seed will lie dormant with its potential for growth inhibited by the conditions surrounding it. As soon as the conditions improve and the soil is nurtured by warmth, moisture and nutrients the seed can begin to draw on its full potential to grow and produce. Nurturing your internal thoughts and guiding your external actions through the use of performance qualities such as positive attitude, an optimistic outlook, and self-direction will offer you the opportunity to draw on your full potential.

The three basic success factors that will determine the level of your achievements are:

Knowledge: you have to know what you're doing.
Skills: you have to know how to do it.
Attitude: knowing how to think positively while doing it.

Of the big three positive attitude, which is one of your performance qualities will be by far the most important factor in determining your success. The relationship between the three factors is somewhat enigmatic in that without knowledge and skills a great attitude isn't going to have much impact on how well you perform the actions needed to generate results. At the same time possessing knowledge and having the skills needed to perform the actions isn't likely to generate much more than average results until the right attitude is used to focus that knowledge and those skills on the most productive actions. Never mistake knowledge for wisdom. Knowledge results from learning. Wisdom is the result of understanding how to apply what you've learned.

For example, a salesperson with above average knowledge and skills, but with a cynical, negative or pessimistic attitude will be held back from attaining the level of success they otherwise would achieve. Lack of determination results in more failure than lack of skills ever will.

Performance qualities like, positive attitude, finding excitement in what you do, seeing yourself as the winner you can be and working with instead of fighting against change can create within you the self-confidence and determination needed to maximize the potential of your knowledge and skills. It comes together to create the stamina you need to stay the course when things get tough. It will help you draw on physical, mental and emotional reserves when needed. Professional selling is a demanding career, you're going to need all three success-factors in peak working order to reach your full potential.

Never Mistake Motion for Action:

Over thirty years of observing salespeople in action has led me to one fundamental conclusion. The success enjoyed by high–achievers, is propelled by the quality of the actions they take and how consistently they take them. The quality of their actions reflects the selling skills they possess. The consistency of their actions is anchored in and driven by their performance qualities. The performance qualities that have the most impact on the success or failure of every professional sales practitioner are:

- Self-Concept
- Internal Motivation
- Self-Confidence
- Personal Values
- Self-Leadership
- Attitude

No matter how well grounded your selling skills are or how much product knowledge you possess, that knowledge and those skills will only produce consistently high results when applied through consistently productive actions. It's in the action phase of the selling process when the real impact of your performance qualities begins to show. Like any other aspect of life professional sales rewards the people who know how to use their skills, not the ones who simply possess them. The selling game rewards the players who do, not those who think about doing. In any game there comes a time when all the planning, practice and theories are put to the test by getting out, doing and making things happen. The selling game is no different.

If the level of your income is linked in whole or in part to commissions or bonuses and is primarily driven by your ability to make sales, let me welcome you to a world where results are what count. Planning to make it happen, thinking about ways to make it happen or hoping to make it happen just doesn't cut it. What does count, is getting out there, putting it on the line, and making it happen.

Everyone who trains for any profession does so with the intention of becoming successful in it. People who train to become professional sales practitioners are no different. You enter a working environment where the road to mediocrity is paved with good intentions. The road to achievement with constructive actions. The world of professional sales is one where results are expected, measured and rewarded. It's a place where competitive people thrive. It's a place for those who like to compete and win. It's a world filled with people who enjoy the challenge of meeting and surpassing goals and objectives. There is no hiding in the shadows in this world. You better be ready to stand in the glare of the spot-light and be judged on the actions you take and the sales you make. You won't survive long hiding behind a facade of what you're planning to do, thinking about doing or promising to get done. What counts and what gets measured, is what gets done.

You can't be successful in this world on I would'a, I

could'a and I should'a. You work in a world where success is driven by I can, I will, and I do. In the final analysis it comes down to this, you make the sale or you don't. You ride the wave of sales made, or drown in a sea of sales lost. Your professional success or failure is judged very simply and clearly on results. Intentions are respected and effort is appreciated, but results are what matter.

So it's important that throughout your sales career and particularly in the early stages of it, you get in the habit of being a hard-nosed, no-holds-barred, honest and objective self-evaluator. No one, particularly when your success is judged on instantly measurable results can afford to waste time waiting and wishing. If you are in the early stages of your selling career an honest straight forward self-analysis of your work ethic and performance qualities can help you get off to a productive start. If you find yourself in an under-achieving sales slump going through the process will help you get back on the right track. You should however always keep this thought in mind; even when you're on the right track you're still going to get run over if you just sit there.

We all have strengths and weaknesses. The key to improved productivity for salespeople is learning how to manage both. It's a given that it's important to make an effort to learn how to use your selling skills in the most productive ways possible. Where a lot of salespeople falter is in spending too much time and energy trying not just to manage their weaknesses but to bludgeon them into submission and banish them from being. Let me suggest that you give up on your mission to eliminate all weaknesses and create the perfect you. Instead learn to start taking constructive actions to improve them and stop beating yourself up over having them. Come to grips with your weaknesses then embark on an incremental journey of self-improvement using a performance quality like your personal values to guide you and keep you focused along the way. You might want to begin your assessment of what weaknesses need to be shored up by evaluating your attitude and your outlook. You might find that you're in need of finding ways to change them from being destructively negative to productively positive.

Negative attitudes and pessimistic outlooks are sneaky little weaknesses that very often lie hidden beneath a lot of the problems of our own making. Too often unsatisfied people forget that you can alter your life by altering your attitude. Putting your focus on finding your own distinctive and personal way to build and maintain a positive attitude and an optimistic outlook can be your first step toward getting off to the right start or out of a selling slump. Another productivity weakness can be the way you react to and deal with unexpected changes and challenges. Do you too often waste time ranting about the unfairness of it all? You can use other performance qualities to better manage the changes around you and learn to take advantage of them by looking to uncover possible opportunities hidden within them. Is one of the weaknesses holding you back a lack of direction in your life? Have you fallen into the trap of going with the flow and allowing your direction to be decided by other people, or situations that seem out of your control? Learning how to become more self-directed and self-confident are performance qualities you can use to overcome that weakness. The stronger your commitment to objective self-evaluation the sooner you will uncover your weaknesses and find ways to manage them and lessen their impact on your performance. In addition as your proficiency at using objective self-evaluation improves you will find it easier and faster to build on your existing strengths.

CHAPTER TWO
Developing a Life Plan

You only live once, but if you do it right that should be more than enough.

You wouldn't think of starting a business without a business plan. Yet most of us start our adult lives without a life plan. Simply put a life plan is designed to get you from where you are, to where you want to be. The first thing to understand is your life plan should not be carved in stone. Your life plan will only be useful in guiding your actions if it is a work in progress. Its primary function will be to serve as a written reminder of how you've decided to conduct your life. It should also serve to fuel your drive and determination to reach your goals and objectives. Think of it as stimulant you can use to energize your commitment to following your path to success.

It doesn't need to be, nor should it be a rigid list of commandments to be followed slavishly regardless of situations or circumstances. It should be written with enough detail to keep you focused on short-term actions, but the key to keeping it practical and viable is to paint your long–term goals in broad-brush strokes. That way you have the flexibility to apply it to changing situations and circumstances as your business and personal life evolves. If your life plan is too detailed you run the risk of having it become just another list of rules and regulations. Society will impose enough of those on you. Your life plan should be a tool for helping you discover your creativity, not stifle it.

You want your life plan to be a motivating driving force when you review it. It needs to contain enough detail of what you want to accomplish, and how you intend to do it, to guide you on your way, but don't let it bog you down by becoming a micro-analysis of every step along the way. There is no point in thinking any of us can ever figure out every eventuality that might occur in our futures. Besides, my experience has been that a lot of what we think isn't going to happen in our lives does and a lot of what we think will, won't. Try looking at your life plan like pilots look at their flight plans. You need to know your starting point and where you intend to land. Then you need to set a course that will get you there with the least amount of turbulence along the way, but you need to have enough flexibility to adjust to any unexpected rough weather you might encounter. Your life plan needs to reflect your genuine belief in what you are capable of accomplishing. One of the many oddities about human nature is that our expectations of what we can or can't accomplish rises and falls in direct proportion to how positively we see ourselves and what we expect from that person we see.

When my daughter was little like a lot of parents we went through the 'I want a gold fish' era. Like any dutiful father I purchased a couple of small goldfish and a fish bowl. The fish had no control over the size of the bowl we placed them in. They did grow a little, but their growth was restricted by the size of their bowl. Unlike those goldfish we do have a choice when it comes to the size of the bowl we want to swim in. The size of the bowl is determined by our expectations of ourselves.

When you expand your expectations you always step up the level of your personal performance. You invariably create new opportunities to generate better results. If you stand on the first tee at the golf club and expect to fumble and bumble your way around the course you probably will. If you think it's hopeless to try to score well, chances are very good, you won't. It works like that when setting your sales expectations and objectives. When you have low personal expectations and set correspondingly low sales objectives you produce lose lose scenarios. Keeping your personal expectations low damages your self-concept. Setting low sales objectives means reaching them still results in low sales production.

One sure fire way to generate average performance is to expect average results. Average is not something you should aspire to, but it is something too many people end up settling for. Setting higher expectations for yourself is the first step in producing above average results. It's like the pygmalion effect in Shaw's play. The best way to become a different person is to think and act like the person you want to become. Keep reminding yourself you have a choice. You can give in and accept the way life is, or you can put together a life plan that includes raising the expectation of who and what you want to be. What have you got to lose?

Remember as stated earlier your life plan works best if you build in some room to maneuver. A completely defined life plan without options locks you into a course of action that can in fact inhibit rather than encourage change. It's the flexibility you build into your plan that makes it different from a list of goals and objectives.

Goals and objectives need to be pragmatic, realistic and attainable to be effective motivational influences on you. Your life plan should also contain elements of pragmatic sensibility, and reality. It definitely must be realistically workable plan. In addition however it needs to be able to help you see and understand the person you need to be to make it work. It needs to be powerful enough to bring you to the point where you can taste feel smell hear and see what living your plan will be like. Developing a productive life plan means going beyond a few wishful thoughts about what could be. To make it an ongoing source of inspiration you need to objectively address issues like:

- Do you need to improve your attitude and if so what steps are you going to take to do it?
- What additional knowledge do you need and where will you go to get it?

- Do you need to improve your skills and which ones in particular will you work on?
- What habits and behaviors are holding you back, and what steps are you willing to take to change them?

Your life plan can't grow in a vacuum. It can only grow stronger in the light of sharing. Share your life plan with the people you love and trust. Encourage them to become active participants in it. When others who share your outlook begin to appreciate your commitment to living your plan they will be drawn to helping you through the process of making it work.

One of the real benefits of having a solid workable life plan is the effect it has on your attitude toward the set-backs most of us encounter from time to time. It helps you put them in perspective and realize that they are only temporary in the overall scheme of things. Any place and time is only temporary in nature when you're committed to moving forward to better things. They serve to point out the current gap between where you are and where you're determined to be. They can also be valuable in helping you judge your performance and identify where improvement is needed.

People without a life plan have a tendency to ignore the big picture. They get hung up on managing the minutia of the moment. When you put all of your thoughts and energy into managing what is instead of working toward what could be you risk spending your time fighting against what you don't want, instead of for what you do. It's counter productive to obsess over what you don't have instead of putting in the effort to go out and get what you do.

If the road to hell is paved with good intentions, then the road to mediocrity is paved with plans that are never implemented. The importance of planning before doing and the benefits to be derived from the exercise is a drum beaten on by every sales manager and sales trainer the world over. I think everyone responsible for managing a sales territory or building a long-term customer base realizes the truth in the message. We all face it seems, an inexhaustible inventory of too much to do and too few hours to do it in workdays. Planning and organizing our priorities is essential in our drive for success, and our need to maintain our sanity. The frenzy to plan and organize however needs to be tempered with the understanding that any plan is only going to benefit the planner if he or she has the determination to implement it consistently and possesses the skills to implement it properly. Any plan without the drive and determination to make it work, is simply an exercise in wishful thinking. It is my considered opinion that success comes to those who spend more time doing what they planned to do and less time planning what they ought to do.

Developing an overall plan for success is not a whole lot different than drawing a trip route on a map. The objective of both is to get from where you are to where you want to be, in the shortest amount of time, over the smoothest roads with the fewest detours. One significant difference is that when we sit down to draw up our plan for success we know no matter how meticulous our plan is there will be unavoidable bumps in the road and detours we will have to take before we reach our destination. It's for that reason we need to include realistically attainable interim goals and objectives along the way. Our interim goals and objectives serve the purpose of keeping us firmly headed down the right roads and in the right direction when we encounter, as we are sure to, people and events that tempt us to take other seemingly easier paths. We all need to see some tangible results from the efforts we're putting in. Without the reward of reaching short term goals and objectives along the way, we lose sight of the long term ones and become easily side-tracked into wandering off course and waste a lot of irreplaceable time doubling back and starting over.

A quick reminder again here, having a plan, writing down your plan, talking about your plan and having the best intentions to follow your plan isn't going to cut it. There is an old Confucian proverb that says; the journey of a thousand miles begins with the first step. Until you take the first step to get started, your plan isn't going to take you anywhere. Your plan has no value until you put it to use. I would be the first to agree that in a typical day filled with the distracting minutia of daily life keeping your eye on the big picture isn't always easy. The daily pressures we all face at home and at work, can cause us to become mired in the moment. It's easy to loose perspective on what is and isn't or should or shouldn't be important. The pace of everyday living can make it difficult to maintain our perspective and focus our attention on following our big picture plan. In our attempt to fit in, be a team player and not rock the boat we too many times end up letting those around us pressure us into putting all of our energy into dealing with the problem de jour.

We get bogged down in trying to do damage control on what went wrong yesterday. This leaves us with little or no time and energy to even think about what we want from tomorrow, let alone plan for it or work toward it. We never seem to commit to stepping off our daily treadmill long enough to afford ourselves the luxury of thinking about, looking toward and doing something about our future. That's why so many of us settle for the sameness of our today's and give up on the promise of our tomorrows. One of the great battles in life is the one fought between trying to be more proactive and less reactive. We would all like to be more in control of the eventual outcome of our lives. We would for sure like to be more controlling of the major and minor aggravations and inconveniences that fill our daily lives. But unless you're living in a hermetically sealed bubble it's not likely to be something that's going to happen. In fact, if we're honest with ourselves most of us will admit that as we sink deeper into managing the daily situations and circumstances that challenge us, we become more reactive to what is happening to us and less pro-active in the making things happen for us. Well thought out, realistic and practical pre-defined short and long term goals and objectives help us maintain a balance between successfully managing and enjoying what we have, while working toward what we want.

Any well conceived series of goals and objectives can act as benchmarks we can use to bring order to our lives while at the same time head us in the right direction and measure our progress along the way. They help us prioritize our time and focus our efforts on the activities we've identified as stepping-stones to our success. They also act as a series of checks and balances to help measure the effectiveness of those activities. I've found that by prioritizing the activities that are going to help me reach my goals and objectives, I spend less time sweating the small stuff and more time on the stuff that will have a real positive impact on my life. Far be it for me to oversimplify life. After all we spend an inordinate amount of time it seems to me, going out of our way to complicate it. Sometimes I think we aren't genetically programmed to enjoy. Even when everything is coming up roses, too many are still too busy looking for non-existent thorns to enjoy the moment.

We are the only species it would seem that hasn't yet concluded that the principal reason for living is to enjoy life. Throw away your hair shirt, life isn't meant to be a test designed to make you stronger for the next one. It's offered to each of us as a chance to enjoy and make the most of each day. My advice is to try combining a series of realistic goals and objectives with a workable plan of action. I predict that in less time than you think the results of your actions will help you break free from any less than satisfying life cycle you might be caught in.

If you want things to be different in your life, you've got to think and act differently. Without a personal plan for success to guide you, the tendency is to drift along doing the same old things and being the same old you. The only way a new you can become different from the old you, is to be willing to think different, act different and be different. In fact if up until now you've failed to be who you want to be, or be doing what you want to do, it's probably the way you've been thinking and doing that has failed you. We don't fail to live up to our potential because of who we are, in most cases we fail because of the decisions we make and the actions we take. Success for a lot of people is closer than you might think. All it takes is the courage and willingness to think and move in new directions. To have any real lasting value any new course of action you set for yourself has to be based on realistically attainable goals and objectives ones that reflect your experience, knowledge and skill set. A good case in point is Michael Jordan's attempted switch from basketball to baseball. He has to be given full marks for being willing to redefine his personal plan for success and make changes to it. However the changes he was trying to make did not reflect the reality of his experience, knowledge and skill set. In the beginning he was energized and highly motivated by the excitement and challenge of the changes he was determined to make. However the shiny luster of new promise began to quickly fade to the pallor of everyday reality. He eventually became frustrated by his inability to attain the personal performance level he demands from himself.

I think the lesson here is that much of what we accomplish has it's beginnings in what we dream of accomplishing. The dream however, has to be able to be transformed into workable reality. Talent in one discipline is not necessarily transferable or easily transferred to another. No matter how extraordinary, talent alone can only take you so far. To take advantage of and maximize the return on the talent we have we need a personal plan for success to guide us. Without a plan to define the best way to use it, our God given or self-developed talent will only carry us so far.

To have value the goals and objectives you work toward need to be concise and specific to your situation. You are going to need a clear unobstructed view of where you want to go before you can feel confident about leaving the safety of where you are. Your new goals and objectives need to stimulate you, excite your senses and ignite your passions. They need to pull you away from your self-imposed and self-limiting comfort zone and away from just making do and toward the promise of what could be and the challenge of making a difference. They should propel you toward your vision of what your future should be.

The single most valuable aspect of developing a life plan for success is this. When driven by well defined and realistically challenging goals and objective it will have a profound impact on empowering and helping you become self-directed. It will give you the direction you need to help you retake control of your life. It places the responsibility for our success squarely on our shoulders, where it belongs. Too many people today lead lives of quiet desperation, putting in time without meaning and effort without direction. When we drift through our lives, without a personal success plan, one we have faith in and control over, we run the risk of becoming spectators instead of players, in the game of life. When that happens we end up having our actions governed and controlled by the situations, circumstances and people that surround us.

CHAPTER THREE
Your Uniquely Individual Self-Concept

Life is like being part of a dog sled team.
If you're not the lead dog, what you see isn't going
to be much to look at.

Success in the world of professional sales demands physical energy, emotional stability and strength. Not the kind of unbending, rigid strength you might associate with an oak tree, but more like the strength of a willow able to withstand the onslaught of rain and wind by bending without breaking. You are bound to go through stretches when your emotional and physical energy are at a low-ebb and your personal values and convictions are put to the test. Every one of you who is intent on new discoveries and raising the level of your performance is going to encounter challenges that at first glance seem insurmountable. When you learn to bend with adversity and not be broken by it you also begin to develop your own personally productive ways of bouncing back from it.

What is it that gives successful people the resiliency to bounce back from adversity when others are sucked under by the same set of circumstances? What provides them with the reserves of energy to stay the course, while others are giving up? The answer lies in developing, maintaining and building on a strong and healthy self-concept. Anyone in a competitive environment needs a secure self–concept to enable you to reach down into your reserves of energy when you need it most. Self–concept is the point at which your self-image, how you see yourself, self–ideal, how you would like to see yourself and your self–esteem, how much you like what you see and like who you are, converge.

The self–concept we develop can when properly nurtured give us an advantage and the edge we need when competing with others. It's one of the factors that will ultimately determine whether or not you push to a level of success above most of your peers or simply decide to settle for being one of the average. Our self–concept helps us determine if the person we are, is capable of doing the things we want to do, and become the person we want to be. If the answer is yes, it becomes the foundation we build on. If the answer is no, it helps us map out a strategy for making the necessary changes to become the person we need to be.

Your level of performance is going to be a direct reflection of the strength of your self–concept. The fact of the matter is, when you feel good about yourself, have confidence in your ability and enjoy what you do, you will create reserves of positive energy that will enable you to sustain higher levels of performance for longer periods of time. When all three are in place you will create more opportunities to raise the bar on your level of personal performance.

Having a strong and healthy self–concept won't take the place of knowledge or skills or the right attitude, but it will give you the positive energy, stamina and stability required to put them all together in a winning package. A strong self–concept helps you cope more easily with life's daily ups and downs. It will help you do less moaning and groaning about the curves that are thrown at you and most importantly you won't find yourself getting bogged down and wallowing in the "poor me" syndrome, so common to people who fail.

The intriguing thing about self–concept is how uniquely personal it is to each of us. You develop over time and through your own experiences the individual self–concept you are going to wear through life. None of us is forced to take the one someone wants us to have. We aren't forced to stand in line and wait for the next available one. Each of us has the freedom, opportunity and responsibility to develop our own. Your self-concept is going to be influenced by your life experiences, your fears, doubts, triumphs, tragedies, likes, dislikes, opinions, ideals and values. All these things contribute to your self-concept. In other words, your self–concept is the sum total of your life's stuff. You are ultimately responsible as keeper of your stuff to decide what stuff you are going to collect, keep and use. Oh sure, if you want to give up and give in, you can let others force their stuff on you. If you do however, the self-concept you wear won't be yours it'll just be a cheap knock-off of someone else's. You can't be a first rate version of yourself, by becoming a second rate version of someone else.

There is one very big advantage to developing your own self-concept based on your own collection of stuff. When the stuff we collect belongs to us, we get to decide what we choose to keep and what we want to get rid of. We can if we choose to get rid of the old out–of–step, self destructive or negative stuff that is holding us back and collect new confidence building, positive stuff that will help us move forward.

Once you realize you're never permanently stuck with stuff the easier it will be to move forward toward who you want to be and what you want to accomplish. My advice is simple, if you find some of your stuff is weighing you down, or holding you back, get rid of it. Too many people without a strong healthy self–concept let others pile a lot of their negative, self-destructive stuff on their shoulders and then convince them it's their job to lug it around. You have the right to decide what kind and how much stuff you choose to collect and carry through life.

Make life's journey easier on yourself. Lighten your load from time to time. Take stock of the stuff you've accumulated. Keep what you need to help you get what you want and recycle the rest. Make a start by tossing out the stuff that drags down your self-concept or confidence and drives up your misery meter. Stuff like, past injustices, bad memories, destructive attitudes. Get rid of those nagging negative thoughts and feelings you might have about people, places or things. Most of all lighten your load by tossing out those self-destructive grudges you've been lovingly caring for, for so many years.

Making quality and lasting changes to anything including your self–concept means being willing to embark on a journey of small incremental steps, requiring time, determination and patience. Like a slow simmering stew, it takes time for new more positive thoughts to flavor our outlook and have an impact on our outward behaviors.

For any of this to work to our advantage we have to face up to and come to grips with a few basic truths. The first is this, what we put into anything determines what we get out. The success of any sales practitioner will be a direct reflection of how well and how often you apply your skills, and do the things that need to be done, when they need doing. The second basic truth is, the only way you can assure yourself of building long-term success is by concentrating your thoughts and actions on those things that are consistent with what you want to accomplish.

It's no secret there is a direct link between concentration and compensation. With the possible exception of politicians, we all know that thoughts precede actions. It's a pretty simple concept. Thinking about positive outcomes helps us concentrate on taking the actions and developing the behaviors needed to make productive things happen. One of the laws of physics states; for every action there is an equal and opposite reaction. My sales practitioner's law states; to generate productive results you need to think positively and work constructively.

It's all about thinking like a winner and acting like a winner. I think most of us have come to realize at some time in our lives that if we aren't prepared to take action and make it happen for us someone or something will make it happen to us. The choice then is, make it happen or wait for it to happen. Let me ask you this though; in the past when you've sat back and waited, have good things come to you, or did you have to go out and get them? I think I would be pretty safe in saying you had to go out and get them. When you sat back and waited for your skills to improve, did they? Not likely! I think most of you would agree that they only improve through practice, trial and error.

When you fold your arms, put your feet up and wait for your self–confidence, self–esteem or self–image to grow and improve do they? I think not! The only way to make a difference is to make the effort. In the world of professional sales, those who make things happen, prosper, those who wait for things to happen, fail.

What about luck you say. Well there's no disputing it's nice to get lucky once in a while. Most of us have had a lucky break or two, but don't you think counting exclusively on luck to see you through is just a tad risky? It means you better be able to figure out how to be in the right place at the right time, a lot of the time. Counting on luck, is not a sure fire formula for success for most of us.

Don't underestimate the power your self-concept can have over your personal productivity. When your self–concept is weak, it's easy to fall into a rut and start to cop out by focusing on just getting through one day after another, instead of making the most of each. When your self-concept is floundering there are bound to be days when you wake up thinking, how come everyone is out to get me, or why is life so unfair. Lets face it those kind of days are not likely to be real stimulating or productive. The reverse happens when your self-concept is alive and well. They are the days you wake up feeling energized, alert and anxious to tackle the issues of the day. The days you look forward to, the days you make the most of, and the days you wish you had more of. They are a direct result of a healthy and secure self–concept. You don't spend those days beating yourself up over what should be, or what might have been. You spend them doing what you need to do to make productive things happen. We all need to remind ourselves from time to time that if we don't believe in ourselves we won't be able to believe in what we can accomplish. The basis of our success lies in our faith in our ability to succeed and we can only maintain that faith by maintaining a strong self-concept. The good news is because we own our self-concept we can make changes to it without having to get anyone's permission. A negative self-concept and the self-defeating attitude and actions that spring from it, don't have to be permanent disabilities. Since we are the creators of our negative thoughts and behaviors we also retain the power to reverse them. The first step is to identify the source of your negativity and then take steps to control or eliminate it. Sometimes it's next to impossible to completely eliminate negative influences in our lives so the next best thing is to learn to control them. By learning to control them we move them from the forefront of our thoughts and push them into the background where they have less impact and influence. Negative thinking and self-defeating behaviors are learned habits and therefore can be controlled, adjusted and over time eliminated. Anyone who has gone through the ordeal of trying to stop smoking knows the time and effort it takes to control and beat a self-defeating habit. Those who are successful appreciate the long-term rewards and benefits of living a cigarette free life. Once you begin to loosen the stranglehold of negative thinking and destructive ways of doing you begin to become aware of the positive possibilities and opportunities that surround you and previously went unnoticed. At the same time your growing self-concept empowers you to reach out and take advantage of them. The rewards of controlling negative thoughts and behaviors and unleashing positives in their place are surely worth the price in terms of time and effort that you are asked to pay.

To begin the process of strengthening your self-concept focus on what's good in your world. Write down the things that for you contribute to a meaningful and happy life. Now write down the things in your life that have contributed to negative and self-destructive thoughts and behaviors. Compare the lists and you may find that some of the same things that have messed you up have been things you have derived pleasure from and have provided you with good times. It's time to make your decision, is the pleasure worth the price? Remember one popular definition of insanity is to keep doing the exact same things in the exact same ways, while expecting different results.

Start to focus your thoughts on appreciating the results of what you accomplish instead of dwelling endlessly on what should'a been or could'a been. Stop beating yourself up over real or imagined mistakes you've made. As long as you're trying to move forward you're going to continue to make a few. When you make them, spend a reasonable amount of time trying to fix them, then as hard as it might be, admit to yourself your not perfect, take off your hair shirt and move on. You're still going to miss the mark on occasion. Instead of dwelling on the misses, get excited about the new opportunities that are open to you. Your world if it's anything like mine, has no shortage of people dwelling in it who welcome the chance to remind you of your shortcomings, mistakes and failures. They'll even do it in most cases without even being asked. Leave it to the doom and gloomsters in your life to live in the past while you move forward into the future. Make a commitment to yourself to open your mind to new objectives and ways to reach them. Always be on the look out for new insights into changing existing ways of doing things. Be willing to accept self or circumstance driven change as an opportunity not an inconvenience.

Make an effort to understand more fully the dynamics of dealing positively with the people around you. Cut people the same slack you expect them to cut you and accept their foibles and idiosyncrasies the same way you expect them to accept yours. Surround yourself with positive and genuine people. Make room in your life for them even if they have differing thoughts and interests from yours. Then try to learn from them and apply what you learn.

In my experience the selling profession is one where the 80-20 rule definitely applies. On almost every sales team I've ever worked with twenty percent of the sales people are exceptional producers while eighty percent are good solid but average producers. If you're not already one of the most productive twenty percent make every effort to get to know them and spend as much time as they will allow you to with them. This accomplished two things, you'll be investing more time with people who can teach you productive habits and wasting less time with people who can't.

Make an effort to consciously think about, talk about and do things that are consistent with your goals and objectives. When you share your ambitions with loyal and trusted friends they can often shed new light on the steps you need to take to reach them. One last thought, when the negative people in your life and make no mistake there will still be plenty of them in it, come to get you, let them have their say, listen to them politely and then ignore them completely.

A quick thought on making decisions.

Professional sales practitioners rarely get a second chance to be right the first time. You're not in a "gimme another chance business". Your ability to make decisions and make them right the first time will have a significant impact on your success and your level of income. Anyone who has ever managed a sales territory will attest to fact that you are called on to make decisions of varying importance everyday.

You can for the most part categorize decisions you are called on to make this way. Some are very significant and have a correspondingly high upside potential or downside consequence. Others are less significant and have a smaller degree of risk and reward. A few are insignificant with little or no risk of long-term damage from being wrong.

When called on to make any significant decision the best course of action is to try to buy some time. Try never to make snap or hurried decisions in the heat of battle. Always try to give yourself some time to think about options and alternative courses of action. Try whenever possible to give yourself the time you need to gather facts and information and get some informed input. Then weigh the possible consequences of your actions from the upside and downside. Do it from your own perspective and that of your customer. But a word of caution here, always be wary of the dangers of paralysis by analysis. My experience has taught me, the best way to make a simple and singular problem multiply is to think too much and do too little. Once you're satisfied that you've thought the situation through and considered all the options, get on with it and make the decision.

You're never going to be right all the time and you're never going to satisfy all of the people all of the time. Your responsibility is to make the decision and live with the result. One other often overlooked aspect of decision making that comes into play for salespeople more so than any other group I can think of is the impact, influence and indeed power of intuition. In spite of your best efforts to formulate the decision making process, and base everything on objective facts and information, do not, I repeat do not, discount your intuition. You're not Mr. Spock so sometimes in spite of the data in front of you, the opinions of others and the thinking you've done, it's best to follow your instincts. Sometimes the decisions we make and the actions we take come down to "ready, aim, fire", or "ready, fire, aim".

CHAPTER FOUR
What's this Selling Game all about?

*In the world of professional sales,
if you can't believe in yourself, you'll have little
chance for success. The basis of your success
will always be your faith in your
ability to succeed.*

I've **been** witness over the years to many successful sales careers and to an equal number of failed attempts. The people who struggle never seem to figure out what is holding them back. Even when offered advice on what to do to turn things around they always seem reluctant to take it. They take the courses, read the books and always seem anxious to learn but they also resist every opportunity to be taught. It's not the product or service being sold that separates them from their more productive colleagues. Many people succeed and many fail while selling the same commodities. It can't be the training they get that makes the difference. Successful and unsuccessful salespeople selling the same things for the same company receive the same training. Nor can you tell by appearance which people are more likely to be successful. I've seen likely fail and unlikely succeed. I've seen people who seemed like they could sell ice to an Eskimo fail, while others who it seemed wouldn't be able to sell a life jacket to a drowning man succeed. I've known people who could recite the latest selling theories and sales techniques verbatim ultimately flounder when facing the challenge of real life selling.

What is it then that makes the difference between those who succeed and others who throw up their hands in frustration? Why is it some salespeople who seem to lack the basic instinct for selling consistently out-perform others who seem to have it? The answer in my opinion is deceptively simple. The ones who find success go looking for it. They don't wait and hope it comes to them. They not only learn, they also respond to being taught. They make an effort to learn the theories and develop their skills, but having done so they get busy putting them into practice. The real difference between top and average producers lies in recognizing the importance of building on a foundation of strong performance qualities. Successful sales professionals don't pay lip service to a performance quality like positive attitude. They believe in it and they live it. They understand the impact it has on the actions they take. They develop their ability to problem solve through another performance quality, creative thinking. They run toward change while others are busy trying to run from it or hide from it. They find a way to be excited about what they do and use that excitement to make a difference while doing it. They use performance qualities like self-direction and self-leadership to set production standards for themselves that surpass what others find acceptable. They have a personal life plan based on productive values. They use it as their internal compass to help them stay on the right path toward their goals and objectives. In addition and this is an under-rated performance quality, they understand the value of seeing their inner winner. They've learned through positive visualizing how to see themselves as winners in winning scenarios. They use all of these and other performance qualities to compliment their selling skills and build up the kind of stamina and resiliency needed to face the daily challenge of professional selling.

The purpose of any selling initiative is to try to stimulate the urge to purchase. The job of every professional salesperson is to point out to prospects and customers that their needs can be addressed most beneficially through the use of your products or services. Ultimately it comes down to convincing your prospects and customers that it is in their best interest to take action, take it now and take it with you. No degree in physics is required to get the sales rocket off the ground. The purpose of selling is easy to understand. The selling process isn't difficult to learn or apply. Everything is simple and straight-forward, nothing here to cause heartburn or acid indigestion. The biggest challenge most salespeople face is finding the perseverance to do what needs to be done, when you may not feel like doing it.

To become successful on any level every salesperson needs to be able to combine various selling skills and personal characteristics in a way that will have a consistently positive impact on his or her prospects and customers. You need to be able to respond to your customer's needs by concisely and accurately describing the features of the product or service you're selling. Then you need to be able to explain to your customers the benefits of using them. You need to know how to ask the right questions at the right time. You need to be able to deliver effective sales presentations to individuals and to groups. Those and other selling skills can be learned and developed through training and first hand experience. Those kinds of skills are a necessary and integral part of any salesperson's tool kit. They are not however in and of themselves the things that are most likely to make the difference between your producing average or above average performance and results.

What you need to add to the mix, are performance qualities. An understanding of how your thoughts control your attitude and your attitude drives your behavior and actions is one example of performance qualities at work. Another is having an awareness of why your self-image and your self-esteem, make up the twin pillars that hold up your self-confidence. You need to appreciate that you can only become a success when you can see yourself being successful.

You need to work at improving your outlook so that you can see the opportunities that are sometimes hidden behind the changes taking place around you. Trying to maintain an above average level of performance while viewing the world around you with a cynical and pessimistic outlook is like trying to walk through a mine-field while blindfolded. You need to practice self-motivation, because that's the only kind that will last and give you the drive and determination to take on new challenges. You need to be able to create goals that are positive motivating influences. You need to understand how interim short-term goals can become energy sources you can burn to fuel the pursuit of your long-term objectives. When you're able to put those and other performance qualities to work along side your selling skills the sum of the parts will definitely make the whole stronger and more successful. Part of the rationale behind my assertion in this book that sales people are made, not born lies in my belief in performance qualities. The fact is, each and every one of you can learn to make better use of your performance qualities the same way you learn how to make use of your selling skills. Professional selling is a marathon not a sprint. A lot of bright, articulate, well–educated and personable candidates who seek to become productive sales professionals miss the mark simply because they don't learn to use their performance qualities to help them muster the resolve to stick it out.

CHAPTER FIVE
Matching the Seller and the Process

Action springs from a readiness for responsibility.

I **am** mindful of the fact bookshelves in every bookstore already bear the weight of hundreds of books written about the selling process and how to apply your selling skills to optimum effect when sitting down with your customers. Those books serve a constructive purpose. They provide their readers with a better understanding of the intricacies involved in a typical selling process and the subtleties of applying their selling skills during that process. They act as a blueprint for how to convert selling theories into practical sales. Any selling process however, is only as good as the salesperson employing it.

The process and the salesperson must be in sync before any selling process can be used to generate consistent results. The qualities of the salesperson have to equal the quality of the selling process. A salesperson might possess knowledge and selling skills but until he or she is able to combine those things with performance qualities like using a positive attitude to look through problems to opportunities or having the self-confidence to break free of self-limiting comfort zones their effectiveness with any selling process will be limited.

Success in any sales driven environment comes from creating selling opportunities and converting those opportunities into completed sales. What you use to consistently convert more of those opportunities into increased sales are knowledge, skills and experience all of which combine over time to become expertise. Even a high degree of expertise isn't going to be enough to keep a salesperson at a peak performance level unless it is matched by performance qualities like self-motivation, self-leadership and self-confidence. Your expertise gives you an advantage over other less skilled or experienced salespeople, but it's your performance qualities that give you the drive and determination to put your expertise to work.

A crucial and under appreciated determining factor separating winners from losers in the selling game is that winners simply have a stronger drive to succeed. That drive feeds off performance qualities like having a positive attitude and an optimistic outlook. You can only work at an optimum productivity level when you feel good about who you are and enjoy what you do. Lack of determination results in more failure than lack of ability ever does. Put simply, to succeed sales practitioners must employ a productive selling process and have the determination to put forth the effort required to take the actions necessary to put themselves in a position to consistently make use of the process.

How important is the person behind the process! One of the greatest tests of courage is to face your fears without losing heart. Learning to recognize and work with your performance qualities will help you to overcome two of the chronic career killers in the world of professional sales. They are prospecting anxiety and fear of rejection. Part of the reason I said earlier that salespeople are made not born is that although you may in fact be born with some of the attributes that can help you make the most of your performance qualities, until you learn to be consciously aware of them and take steps to maximize their development they will remain untapped resources. If you don't make the effort to learn how to put them to use, you will almost certainly find yourself mired in mediocrity and wondering why. This is not to say that if you don't learn to work with your performance qualities you're destined for failure. What it means is that it will make it more difficult if not impossible for you to reach your full potential and enjoy the level of success your efforts entitle you to. It is essential to understand how various performance qualities such as an active positive attitude and an optimistic outlook can be interwoven with others such as self-leadership to generate inner-driven and self-motivated determination. Or, how being able to visualize your inner-winner helps you uncover the opportunities hidden in the challenges you face.

In any sales-driven environment it is the development and consistent application of selling skills alongside performance qualities that will play a key role in separating those who get by from those who reach the top. If your intention is to rise above the average success level and corresponding income level of most of your peers you need to focus on two distinct aspects of the challenge. Firstly, you need to make every effort to continue to learn, apply and improve productive selling skills. (It seems an odd paradox but in my experience it's always the best that want to get better. In every group of sales professionals I've ever been associated with, it's the top people who have enough respect for themselves and dedication to achieving their goals, who invest in themselves by investing in education, personal growth and skills development.) Secondly, you need to make an effort to increase your understanding of how your performance qualities can help you make more efficient and effective use of your skills. A working knowledge of selling skills will strengthen the process of making the sale. A comprehensive understanding of personal performance qualities will fortify the person behind the process.

You rob yourself of the opportunity to fully develop your potential when you take the time and put in the effort to improve your selling skills without taking the additional step to make an effort to fully develop the person applying them. As I mentioned, knowledge is one essential ingredient on which to build a strong foundation for success. It is up to you to turn that knowledge into the skills you need to make the most of who you are. It's the inner you that fuels the drive and determination you need to find a way around or over the obstacles that life has a habit of challenging you with. It really is what's inside that counts and helps you keep on keeping on, when others are bailing out.

To some of you reading this book, and discovering the concept of the impact performance qualities can have on your success the whole idea may seem at first glance abstract, vague and far removed from the chaos of your daily battles to slay the dragons. They do however play a pivotal role in your successes and failures. When you understand them and develop their potential within you they will provide you with a heretofore-untapped advantage. They will over time become one of the allies you count on most in your drive to succeed. As you become more aware of them they will provide you with a reservoir of endurance, perseverance and uncompromising determination you can call on when needed.

I believe success in selling anything to anybody must begin with a primary understanding of human nature. Having at least a rudimentary understanding of what makes both you and your customers tick is fundamental to your success. It's a two-part process. Understanding why your customer's respond either positively or negatively to you, and your selling process is essential and can be learned in any sales training program. Understanding yourself through self-evaluation of your strengths and weaknesses is equally important. This part of the process is seldom addressed in detail in traditional selling skills training programs which tend to emphasize the first part of the process while glossing over the second. I would argue that until you are able to analyze and dissect your own patterns of thinking and behavior you won't be in a position to take the appropriate approach to presenting your product or service to the diverse types of customers that make up your customer base.

The single common denominator that is held constant in any life situation, whether the context is at home, work or play, is our own undeniable presence. We are the person we spend all of our time with. We are undeniably the center of our own little universe. We are therefore the person we need to have a positive working understanding of. The first step in the process of developing a positive working relationship with our inner selves is to accept the fact that the level of success we achieve in life will not be determined or controlled by luck, fate, circumstances, situations or the people around us. We will determine it through our thoughts and actions. We are the ones most responsible for what happens to us. We determine our successes and failures. Therefore we are the ones charged with the responsibility to inspire the positive thoughts we need to help us take the productive actions that drive our success. Those positive thoughts, productive actions and constructive behaviors are most often the result of knowing how to create and maintain performance qualities like self-motivation and self-leadership. The bottom line on this one is, we are the person in our lives most responsible for helping or hurting ourselves.

Every selling process is unique to the person applying it. Any productive selling process is a combination of what the salesperson brings to the table in terms of product knowledge, theoretical training and practical experience combined with uniquely personal attributes and characteristics. It's the inner person behind the outward personality that makes every salesperson and selling process distinctly individual.

It's never easy to acquire new skills, and it takes work and dedication to learn and apply the myriad of skills needed by today's selling professionals. This is especially true for people getting into the game late, or coming from other sectors where sales wasn't part of their responsibility. The real challenge these people face however, lies in developing the personal performance qualities they will need to adjust to the daily ups and downs of working at a job that demands consistent results, in order to generate consistent income. Selling is all about moving forward to the next sale, with little time to bask in the glow of the last one. It takes an understanding of how to get the most out of your performance qualities to be able to maintain the energy level needed to sustain long–term success.

Selling is an individual sport wrapped in a team game. Salespeople more so than most are team–centric individuals. They revel in their individuality while enjoying the camaraderie of being part of a sales team. They enjoy competing with other team members for top spot on the team as much as they enjoy beating the competition. In addition to being charged with the responsibility of generating their own sales driven income salespeople in almost every case have the additional mandate of contributing to the success of a sales team.

One of the aspects of being a salesperson I enjoyed most over the years was the chance to be part of a team. Being a productive member of a winning sales team is different from say being the bean counter of the month in the accounting department. The camaraderie shared and the war stories told by my colleagues on the sales teams I was privileged to be part of is something I miss. I always felt it gave me a unique opportunity to blend my talents with others on the team. It also offered a chance to test my talent and measure the results of my efforts against those of my teammates in a competitive but friendly team environment.

I am a baseball fan of the first order. I've always been fascinated by what I see as the similarities between a team of baseball players and a team of sales professionals. Baseball is a team game that stresses individual excellence. A player's true value can be assessed in part by his individual accomplishments as in personal production and in part by his contribution to the team in terms of helping to reach overall team objectives. A winning team is usually comprised of a few top players supported by a cast of average and above-average contributors. Every player begins the season with a list of individual goals and objectives. Every team begins each year with one simple objective win more games than the competition. When enough individuals on a team reach their personal objectives the likelihood of the team winning becomes much greater. Conversely the success of the team greatly enhances each individual players chances for personal success. The relationship between team and individual success seems to follow in most cases a very clear, linear path either upward or downward. An example would be a pitcher who begins the year with an individual objective of winning twenty games. That pitchers individual objective in spite of his best efforts is unlikely to be met unless the team plays a strong supporting role.

The same holds true for salespeople. Individual success will heighten team success and team success will contribute to the success of the individual. Each individual salesperson can only be successful by using his or her talent and skills in productive ways. The same individual to team relationship exists in every sales group I have ever been a part of. Productive salespeople are always more productive when they are part of a winning sales team. Success is contagious. The more you win, the more you want to win and the more you will win.

Why do some salespeople struggle so much with the team concept that is such an integral part of professional selling? It can happen for a number of reasons, but most struggle because their ego works against them. Like most athletes who reach the pinnacle in their sport, salespeople who attain high levels of achievement carry with them to the summit some pretty strong egos. There is nothing inherently wrong in believing in yourself and practicing self-actualization. The danger is in letting your ego take flight to the point where you become totally self-absorbed and start believing in your own infallibility. That's the point where your actions become detrimental to you and others around you. We've all encountered people like that, they're the ones who when we finally do discover the center of the universe are going to be sadly disappointed.

Instead of working with the people around them they work on their own agenda to the total exclusion of anyone else. You see this exemplified in salespeople who are resistant to sharing with colleagues who are part of their sales team. They are always on the periphery never quite fully participating in team initiatives. They are consumed with personal gain and individual recognition. They don't work with colleagues they work around them. These people seek to work outside accepted company parameters and to defy conventional proven ways of generating results. They want to reinvent the wheel. Their egotism leads them to believe what has been learned through time, trial and error and proven by others to be the most effective and efficient way of selling their company's product or service won't work for them. Why won't it work for them? It won't work for them because as they will tell anyone who makes the mistake of asking, they're different. They let their ego convince them that there's a better way for them and them alone to do it. They start believing they shouldn't be expected to be encumbered by proven procedures. They'll find their own path.

Unconventional innovative thinking the kind that leads to positive change is generally something most people find commendable. Most admire those who have the ability to think outside the box. Yet, when innovation is used for the sake of personal expediency it loses its cache. When unconventional methods of doing things are sought simply for the sake of individuality and being different the reason behind the purpose loses validity. Anyone can be creative and innovative when there are no boundaries. The truly creative and innovative learn to improve the results of their efforts within established boundaries. When the top salespeople in your company all follow similar patterns and have managed to generate consistently high sales there would seem to me to be more upside to following their example than there would be in charting your own unproven course. I am not suggesting everyone get out their crayons and start coloring exclusively inside the lines all of the time. It does seem to me however that trying to replicate the successes of the people who have already been there and done that is a creative challenge in it's own right. You still have the creative freedom to be as ambitious as you want to be, with the added advantage of bringing innovative individuality to an established blueprint for success.

CHAPTER SIX
Managing Negativity

*An optimist has more fun being wrong
than a pessimist ever does being right.*

Negativity, cynicism, skepticism and pessimism are the four horsemen of the sales world's apocalypse. Unchecked they can grow and take over your thoughts like weeds taking over an unattended garden. Like weeds they have the ability to blend in so that the damage they do goes unnoticed until too late. What makes it so difficult for most of us outside of the ordained clergy to really keep negativity at bay is the absurdity of a lot of what daily life serves up. I mean it's not easy not to be skeptical about some of the comings and goings of most of the people enjoying their fifteen minutes of fame.

I try very hard not be cynical about politicians and their agendas but I think doing so would test the faith of the sainted. Like the weeds in your garden control rather than eradication of your negativity is your best course of action. It is probably best to make an honest effort to control your negativity, cynicism, skepticism and pessimism rather than putting too much focus on, putting too much effort into and taking too much time to try get rid of them completely. A lot of what we laugh at has its roots firmly planted in cynicism and skepticism.

How you might ask; can things that are so primary to what most of us find so funny be bad for us? I don't have the answer. To me it's always been one of the great ironies, right there with why most of the really good tasting foods we eat, shouldn't be eaten. The cost of negativity is high. One of the real tests of courage is to face defeat without losing heart. Even the most positive among us if they are positive realists will admit to having occasional negative reactions to some situations or having the odd cynical thought. Some occasional negative thinking is pretty normal and not really harmful. Negativism in the extreme is. Consistent, continuous and self-perpetuated negative thinking will invariably lead to self-impeding behavior and all too frequently results in self-destructive professional and personal choices.

Too many skeptics put too much of their energies into proving attitude can't alter their lives. I have a brother who is one of the great cynics of the ages. He has a cynically negative take on almost everything and sees sinister agendas and conspiracies behind almost everything. Yet he is also one of the funniest people I know and is well liked by friends and colleagues. He channels his cynicism and negativity most often into humorous observations about the goings on in the world around him. He is the guy in the conversation who can always be counted on to insert some gallows humor into the subject being discussed. He is an example what I call negative normalcy. He enjoys the cool of negativity and the reaction from others to his biting and cynical quick quips. He is a factory worker and as such he can afford to air his views for all to hear. He isn't going to be held back from promotion because of his negative attitude and he wouldn't be in line for promotion if he changed his cynical outlook. In his job what he thinks or says has no impact on the hourly rate he is paid. He like so many others is putting in his time doing what he does, because of having to, not wanting to do it. He chose early on not to risk the disappointments that are an inevitable part of searching for opportunity. He opted instead to settle for the certainty of whatever was easy. Those who know my brother well know him to be a nice guy who would give you the shirt off his back. He is fair in his dealings with people. He is a people person who enjoys the company of like-thinking friends. In other words his negativity is pretty normal for anyone who chooses to take the path he chose. It influences his attitude about his life and his outlook on what life offers him and at times it will affect his actions toward the people around him. On the whole though his is a live and let live attitude.

He may be self-defeating but he doesn't take overt actions to make life difficult for those who aren't. He doesn't try to undermine the positive determination of others around him, he simply can't bring himself to admit attitude can make a difference. He doesn't demand much from himself and doesn't expect much from people around him. He is a settler. He learned to settle for what life puts on his plate. He lives what most of us would consider a normal everyday non-challenging life. He goes to work he supports his family on an average income and aspires to nothing more. I think we all know at least some people like him, because they make up the vast majority of people in this world. They don't buy into the belief that attitude can make a difference or that it's possible to change their situation by taking constructive actions. They are content to take what life dishes out and get by without taking on the challenge of personal ambition. My brother and millions of others like him are fortunate in one way. They find themselves doing jobs where their attitude doesn't directly influence their income. Professional salespeople aren't so lucky. You cannot aspire to climb to the top in your profession while carrying the weight of negativity, cynicism, pessimism and skepticism on your shoulders.

Some people it seems really are their own worst enemies. They are the people who given a choice always choose to look at the dark side of any situation. They wallow in pessimism and self-pity. They victimize themselves, or go out of their way to put themselves into situations where they can claim they've been victimized. Their thoughts are mired in doom and gloom. In their conversations they focus on and repeat whatever the latest negative news might be. These are people who find themselves trapped in a continuous cycle of unhappiness and despair brought on by their thoughts and actions, and yet blame everyone and everything around them for their plight. They make every effort to convince themselves they are destined to fail and they work very hard at fulfilling their self-constructed prophecy.

They are always so busy finding fault with people and circumstances and looking for people and things to blame for their failure they never take the time to step back and figure it out. The more skeptical they are about their own abilities the more pessimistic they are about their opportunities. The more negative they are about their circumstances and the more cynical they are about people the more likely they will be to continue to fail. Their failure is inevitable and bound to continue because when faced with chances to make changes in their situation, or take on challenges that will lead to altering it, they condition themselves to think first about the likelihood and consequences of failure. This results in fear of and avoidance of new opportunities. Then they simply continue to repeat the actions they are comfortable with, but which cause them to continue to fail.

When we continue to put our energy into thoughts that build the kind of imaginary fences that keep our fears in and opportunities out the results are predictable. Confining our thinking to dwelling on worst-case scenarios is not very likely going to create positively energy. It's inevitable that in a surprisingly short time all of that self-defeating worst-case thinking will manifest itself through the development of negative behaviors and self-destructive actions. We find ourselves searching out and spending time with others who share an equally self-destructive outlook. One of the fist steps in breaking out of the clutch of negativity is to take a look at the people we surround ourselves with. If we take some time to step back and think about and make an effort to understand how much of an impact people around us can have on our ideas, attitude, behaviors and actions we can begin to make conscious decisions about what kind of people we want influencing us. We may not be able to choose family, but we do have a choice in the matter of friends and work colleagues. We can choose to surround ourselves with people who can contribute to and strengthen our determination to succeed. We do have a choice. Do we want people around us we can admire and who inspire, or do we want to surround ourselves with others whose energy has turned to lethargy and whose aspirations have become blurred and buried. We all can't be heroes, someone has to stand on the curb and clap as they go by, but we have the choice of being one of those marching or one of the others standing and watching.

I'm certain everyone reading this book will relate to what I am about to say next. The negativism that surrounds some people is almost palpable. I'm sure you've experienced at least one instance when you've been with someone or in a group of people and sensed the lethargy and almost been able to reach out and touch the indifferent aura surrounding them. They show little or no drive, determination or ambition and they exhaust you with their constant whines of self-pity like these:

- The job I'm in never really turned out like I thought it would, but it's too late to do anything about that now.
- I could do what it takes to be one of them, but why would anyone want to work that hard.
- There's no way I'm selling myself out to be successful, like they do.
- I've got other more important things to spend my time and talents on.
- I don't know where they get the energy, I'm tired before I get out the door in the morning.
- It wouldn't be hard to make that kind of money, if I got everything handed to me like they do.
- Things would be different for me if.
- No sense trying anything new, it's just going to turn out to be more of the same.

As a reformed cynic and ex practitioner of self-indulgent negativism I understand first hand the challenge faced when attempting to develop and maintain a positive attitude and optimistic outlook. If it was easy, it wouldn't be as highly prized a commodity or as worthwhile having one. Since the majority of people we are going to interact with will almost always be more negative than positive, we face subtle but constant pressure to conform and be like them. Misery it is true, loves company. When you conduct your life based on pro-actively looking for the good in situations and people instead of reacting negatively to everyone and everything you are going to be branded as being different. You seldom respond to situations and challenges the way others might. Any of you reading this who have been through it will understand when I say there is an almost perceptible pressure today to give in and do what everyone else is doing and think the way your friends and peers are thinking. Be a joiner, don't rock the boat, be a team player, c'mon just fit in and get by, don't try to stand out and make a difference.

The world around us is a powerful conditioner. Those of us who try to maintain an optimistic outlook face the same negative bombardment as those who choose to give into it. A lot of everyday life we encounter saps our positive resources. The media we watch, read and listen to seems to re-affirm the proliferation of negatives in the world around us. The information flow that is so much a part of our daily lives is inundated and fixated on the negative. Newspapers sell on bad news, television and radio are mired in negativity and seem driven to compete with each other for who can report first or give the most detailed in depth analysis on the most shocking stories of malevolent human behaviors. Accounts of everyday accomplishments vie for space among the stereo ads on page fifteen, while examples of greed and suffering fill the first page headlines. The drumbeat continues everyday. What's the point, just do what it takes to get by. You can't make a difference why bother.

To overcome the overtures of negative people inviting us to join them and play in their sand-box, we have to set out on a separate less traveled path. A path of self-discovery. One that will lead us to our own truths about what we in our hearts and minds believe. One that will help us find the courage to question the popular wisdom and think for our-selves. We have to find ways to counteract the messages that others try to influence us with. One of those ways is by becoming the authors of our own messages. We need to begin sending positive and optimistic inner voice messages or mind–memos to ourselves. Messages that reflect our enjoyment in being who we are. Ones that build our pride in what we do and the way we do it. Those are the kinds of messages that when combined with a performance quality like self-leadership instill in us the pride we need to give us the determination to break out and go beyond being average.

A lot of the people around you drag themselves down to the safety and security of being average because they don't want to have to put in the effort to stand out. They settle for becoming average because at sometime in their lives they make the conscious decision to sell out to the ease of under-achievement. These ordinary everyday people are content to just get by, follow the pack and fit in. There are lots of jobs where these people can toil in obscurity, satisfied to do what it takes to get through the next job review and collect what-ever the annual increase might be. Professional selling isn't one of them. Sales professionals don't enjoy that luxury.

When the level of your income and the quality of your life style are based primarily on the result of your efforts to make sales, you can't afford to settle for average. You have to find a way to raise the level of your performance. In order to do that you have to find a balance between fitting in with your customers and standing out from the people you compete with. One way to do it is to use a performance quality like a positive attitude to manage problems and uncover the opportunities often hidden within them. You can approach a problem in one of two ways. The least productive is to scurry around looking for someone to blame. The most productive way to manage any problem is through positive intervention and action. Instead of channeling your thoughts, reactions and energy exclusively into who or what caused the problem, look for solutions. Solving the problem will satisfy your customers need for a solution and can often lead to increased business. Affixing blame doesn't satisfy the need to fix the problem now or in the future. In addition with a pessimistic or negative attitude you are much more likely to focus on avoidance of facing the problem and procrastinate with your response. When you are trying to build long-term loyal customer relationships this can only lead to missed opportunities, poor customer relations and failure. Once again we have to remind ourselves that attitude determines actions. Without the attitude needed to commit to facing our problems head on we inevitably find ourselves trying to avoid the responsibility of confronting them and dealing with them.

A positive attitude and optimistic outlook will impact on another significant aspect of your selling activities. Without them you will begin to overestimate the risks associated with new challenges and end up missing out on the opportunities that come from facing up to them, and managing them correctly. You might look at a prospective customer and decide that for whatever reason you have little or no chance of doing business with them. The result is, you convince yourself not to bother risking the time and effort to make a prospecting call. Without a positive way of thinking and a constructive way of doing we end up putting too much emphasis on the risks and not enough on the rewards. You begin to convince yourself the best course of action is action avoidance. Of course for any sales professional that leads directly to a slump in sales. On the flip side, a positive and optimistic attitude will provide you with the self–confidence and determination to take on the risks that create the opportunities that result in increased probabilities for success.

That's one of the reasons positive reinforcement from inside and out can make such a difference in our performance and has such a powerful impact on us. Johnny Miller, one of the most talented and successful golfers of the past fifty years tells a great story about the impact of positive reinforcement in his life. His dad began coaching him when Johnny was only seven years old, and continued to be his only coach until he turned twelve and entered a junior golf program. They would spend hours together practicing the mechanics of the game, the swing, the grip, the stance and the follow through. What Miller remembers most was the unbridled enthusiasm his father had for the game and the consistently positive reinforcement he offered to him. Miller claims that without his dad's positive encouragement he would never have enjoyed the experience of learning the skills needed to become the exceptional golfer he is and more importantly he would never have been able to endure the long hours of practice necessary to perfect his skills.

Too often, throughout out lives the feedback systems used to determine our success are based less on reinforcing what we accomplish and more on reminding us of what we don't. Beginning in our early schooling and continuing through our working careers we are most often measured against arbitrary standards of behavior and accomplishment and judged by how far we fall short of the mark. The feedback we get can sometimes be couched in positive language but the bottom line is, we too often walk away not feeling good about what is, but instead inadequate based on what could have been. Consequently a lot of people figure out pretty quickly that only a very few ever even come close to reaching the top and promptly give up. At about the same time they learn how little effort it takes to get by and generate average acceptable results and that becomes their benchmark. It's easy, it's reachable, it doesn't take a lot of effort and the rewards are adequate. The feedback systems prevalent in school and business without meaning to almost always stifle individual creativity and risk-taking by encouraging people to avoid the damning consequences of failure instead of striving for the positive rewards of excellence.

Chapter Seven
Avoid Communication Breakdown

There is nothing more annoying than someone talking while you're busy interrupting.

There are as many different types of selling situations, as there are various types of salespeople. I have always been involved in sales scenarios where the key to consistent productivity was repeat business. I sold my products to buyers who represented companies within my sales territory. Whomever you sell your product or service to, if repeat business is part of your objective the act of communicating with your customers will be vitally important to your level of success. When your type of selling requires consistent contact with your customer base your objective is two fold. One, to continue selling additional goods and services to them and two, earn the right to ask for referrals to other potential customers.

Positive interaction between people lies at the center of productive communicating. Selling is very much about productive communicating between the seller and the buyer. The fact these interactions between people can take place in business or social-situations doesn't change the basic dynamic. Positive communication depends to a large extent on the people involved 'clicking'. All of us possess and interact using certain communicating characteristics. Every sales practitioner encounters an infinite number of communication styles among his or her prospects and customers. The best salespeople know how to adjust and adapt and react productively to a whole cross section of communication characteristics.

Some people are essentially relationship oriented. These people most often communicate in a friendly, low-key unhurried way. They don't use an overly assertive style when communicating. They usually let others dictate the pace and intensity of any conversational interaction. People with these communicating characteristics, are often described by others as being agreeable and supportive. Some people communicate in almost the opposite way. They are action oriented fast paced talkers who are often described as being assertive. Others people may be more thought oriented and communicate in a cautious and studious way. They appear to others as being orderly and persistent. Still others communicate using energetic and enthusiastic characteristics. The people they communicate with often describe them as being ambitious and fun to interact with. None of these common ways of communicating is any more or less advantageous than another. If you don't have a basic under-standing of your communicating characteristics however, they can restrict your ability to reach out to others who possess different ones. An action-oriented communicator may have great results when interacting with someone who possesses the same type of communicating characteristics. They mesh right away and communication barriers disappear quickly.

They are quick to find a comfort level with each other based on the commonality of the way they communicate. You can see however based on they way they communicate that they may have an uphill climb in store when trying to find a comfort level with say someone who has a more analytical and less assertive style of communicating. One may see the other as being pushy, too dominating and overly aggressive. While the other may go away thinking they've encountered someone who is indecisive and too picky about seemingly insignificant details. If you want to reach out effectively to a wider range of people with communication characteristics that differ from yours try doing two things. First take an objective look at the way you communicate and come across to people. Decide which characteristics are dominant in the style you use when communicating with others. Then think about how those characteristics can be tempered when necessary to mesh with people who use differing ones. Flexibility in thinking and doing are the keys.

Finding a common way of communicating with your customers is the ideal starting point to move forward from when attempting to establish long-term productive business relationships. You may find one of the reasons you aren't reaching your sales objectives is because you haven't developed a flexible enough approach to communicating with your customers.

Any communication between two people is always made up of three distinctive and possibly contentious parts. The first is what the person speaking thought they were saying. The second is what the person being spoken to thought they were hearing. The third part is what was actually said. It's amazing how a seemingly simple exchange of words between two people can be fraught with so much potential danger.

In terms of productive communicating, we haven't really advanced all that much through the ages. Where once we sat around the cave gazing at the fire and grunting at each other, we now sit clustered around the television, our conversation restricted to two-minute sound bites during commercials. Like communication itself, communication barriers can come in many guises. When communication breaks down it's very often no one person's fault but for a sales professional a breakdown in communication can very quickly become a very damaging problem.

In the early years of human evolution survival depended on group strength, closing ranks when danger appeared and building barriers to keep intruders at bay. Ironically, the professional survival of modern day salespeople is the antithesis of that. Instead of building barriers sales professionals must become adept at taking them down. Their survival is all about learning how to find ways to communicate productively with a diverse customer base. Instead of closing ranks, professional sales people must be individually skilled team players. Their success is tied to the success of their customers and colleagues. Cooperation in building productive customer relationships is the order of the day. Sharing expertise and working closely with others is necessary for everyone to reach shared objectives. The best way to get what you want is to help others get what they want. That means finding ways to build bridges to replace barriers.

We all have our own perspective on things and our own unique ways of responding to them. This often results in two outwardly similar people responding to seemingly similar situations, circumstance and challenges in very different ways. A lot of the communication barriers people encounter are the result of and stem from differences where, when and how we were brought up. The attitudes we carry, the opinions we offer and the views we hold dear have been crafted by our life experiences going all the back to childhood. It's those experiences along with current influences that shape and guide us. Successful people have the flexibility in thinking to adjust their attitudes, opinions and views when changes around them warrant it. The less successful continue to live by the self-limiting credo, the more things change, the more I will remain the same.

We all live in our own unique world and travel private roads. For that reason it's true that rarely do two people ever think exactly alike. The opinions and values that you hold to he sacrosanct and the logic you use to apply them, may seem eminently just and fair to your way of thinking but may not be as enthusiastically embraced by others around you.

Communication can break down or a conversation may go off the rails in any number of ways. It can happen when one person can't relate, because of differing life experiences, to the logic of the other's point of view. Or, it may be the result of one person feeling their uniquely personal value system is being compromised or threatened by the other. Although most people are generally accepting of the old adage 'to each his own', a lot of people continue to fall into the self-righteous trap of 'my way or the highway'. Lack of fundamental agreement on the source of a problem and the right way to deal with it can be a cause of communication breakdown. Having both parties re-visit the problem and work objectively toward a mutually acceptable solution will usually repair this common communication breakdown.

A much more serious breakdown can occur when because of differing communication characteristics one party to a discussion feels the other is attacking them personally or does not respect the validity of their opinion. We all act defensively when we feel our point of view is not being taken seriously or our value system is being compromised.

Consider this example. I might be having a conversation with you based on a topic I consider to be pretty mundane and straightforward, yet that same topic might in fact be very volatile and charged with emotion for you. Why would we have such diverse opinions on the same topic? Differing life experiences, that's why. One way to overcome our tendency to think our point of view is universally shared by all right thinking people is to be more empathetic to other's points of view. Try to make a genuine effort to see the logic and value in the other side of the issue. Have the same respect for other people's opinions that you expect them to have for yours. In order to accommodate divergent opinions without insult or injury to either party in a discussion it is important to remain open to all types of reasoning. Being genuinely open to and respectful of differences of opinion can knock down commu-nication barriers, broaden your perspective and even help you learn a thing or two.

We all receive input on everything we think about from both our hearts and our heads. Communication breakdowns occur most frequently when the balance between the two goes out of whack. When one or the other of our emotional or intellectual perceptions becomes too dominant we are unlikely to be able to respond to situations clearly and fairly. We will in a lot of cases respond inappropriately and take incorrect action. Thinking too logically without emotion, or too emotionally with little or no logical input blinds us to alternatives and binds us to our carved in stone positions.

Drawing lines in the sand can only lead to participating in all or nothing confrontations, instead of a finding common-ground solutions through candid conversations. Communicating is not about competing it's about co-operating. One small step in becoming more open and receptive to other opinions, ideas and thoughts is to make an effort to keep your eyes and ears open more and your mouth open less. It's always to your advantage to listen closely and explore the other person's point of view before offering your own.

Sales professionals become much better communicators when they realize selling is less about convincing and more about understanding. I think I would be right in saying most of us have walked away from at least a few volatile situations convinced we had won the argument, but realizing we had also lost the sale. Even when you find yourself discussing a topic that is near and dear to you and one you feel a strong emotional attachment to, it will still be to your advantage to listen closely to and explore the other person's point of view. Remember there are three sides to every story, yours, the other person's and the objective facts. All too often in times of stress we seem to conveniently forget the latter two.

You can often diffuse the emotion that accompanies conflict of opinion by making an effort to find a common ground on which to build mutual understanding. One way to accomplish this is to admit your own emotional subjectivity. Taking the lead and admitting you find it difficult not to be emotionally tied to the subject being discussed can have a dramatic impact on the tone of the discussion. In effect you are admitting your fallibility and most fair-minded people are likely to be disarmed by your admission. This in turn will ease the emotional tension and broaden the opportunity to compare both subjective and objective points of view calmly and clearly. Your resolve to communicate and not compete is usually put to the test when customers call you to complain about a problem with your product or service. These problem-solving exercises are often the true test of your communicating skills. Perhaps there's a problem with the performance of your product, or the deliveries are consistently late whatever the reason, regardless of what the situation is it requires fast and satisfactory resolution. Every customer concern represents an opportunity to prove your commitment to a customer-first way of doing business or if not handled correctly the first step in customer dissatisfaction leading to the loss of that customer.

Problem situations with customers can be managed most effectively when you avoid the temptation to get defensive which invariably leads to the hunt for someone to blame. Your focus needs to be on how to resolve the situation to your customer's satisfaction. Make every effort to be empathetic to your customer's concern while suggesting to them that it is everyone's best interest to fix the situation, not affix the blame. By setting aside the hunt for who is to blame, you can put the onus on the positive steps that need to be taken to solve the problem and get your working relationship back on track. While you must always demonstrate your concern for the welfare of your customer, it does not reflect well on you to cow-tow to their every whim and picayune complaint. Salespeople always walk a fine line between customer service and company loyalty. Sometimes the customer isn't always right and in those cases you need to stand up for the integrity of your company, even at the risk of having a customer walk away.

Most good communicators are also adept at influencing the way others think. In my opinion there is a very big difference between being able to positively influence someone or manipulate them. Manipulation is usually used for the purpose of getting your own way at the expense of others. Constructively influencing the thoughts and actions of others to help them generate productive results is beneficial for everyone. We all influence each other in subtle and not so subtle ways everyday. We are trying to influence how others feel about us when we say positive things about them or do nice things for them. "Do unto others as you would have them do unto you", influences us to take positive actions toward others. "What goes around comes around", is an influential warning of what might come to be, if we don't. I'm honest enough to admit that when I buy a nice birthday gift for my wife I'm trying to have a positive influence on our relationship.

I like to think my reason for doing good things for people is altruistic but in my heart of hearts I know I'm also hoping they will reciprocate in kind. The fact of the matter is that when you go out of your way to have a positive influence on people's thoughts and actions you are likely in most cases to gain some personal benefit. I don't think knowing that should make us feel guilty about doing it. When good people do good things for other good people the result can only be good for everyone. I didn't realize what I was doing at the time but I used to try to be a positive influence on the way my dad felt about lending me the family car by keeping it washed and polished. At the time I just figured the better his mood the more miles I got to put on the car.

My contention is that when the objective is to influence others to think positively and act constructively and the results achieved are beneficial to everyone then influencing others by the way you communicate with them is a good thing. If you have confidence in the quality of your product or service, and are convinced your prospective customers have both a need for it and can benefit from using it then there exists justification for doing everything you can to sell it to them. Your obligation is to influence them to take actions that will benefit them. That's part of what professional selling is all about.

It always comes down to results. A good working relationship between customer and salesperson can be built on any number of things from casual common interests to trust, shared benefits, information and expertise, or fulfillment of needs. The one undeniable fact however is that the core strength of every mutually-beneficial long-term business relationship is built on results. The kind of results that not only meet the customer's needs but also exceed their expectations. A customer doesn't care about your good intentions to deliver on time, or fix a problem, or return their calls as promised. They care about whether or not you do it. There is no half–way mark when dealing with your customers. You either deliver results or you don't. In the world of competitive professional sales intentions have no value, as currency, the coin of the realm is results. It may not be fair and it may not be just but the reality is this; professional salespeople are judged by the customers they work with solely on the basis of their actions, not their intentions. Your chances to generate repeat sales with any customers increase significantly when you act in accordance with their needs, and match your actions to your intentions.

Therefore, it is vitally important that your thoughts, behaviors and actions be focused on getting positive results for your customers. The quantity of positive responses you receive from your prospects and customers will be a direct reflection of the quality of the information and service you provide, along with the way it's provided. You won't have to wait for your performance to be judged. Your customers always provide ample feedback for a job well done, or one that could have been done better. The level of their buying speaks volumes.

The only way you can hope to have others respond positively to you is by consistently exhibiting the kind of attitude and taking the kind of actions that helps them see and experience your enthusiasm for what you do. Consider this, would you prefer to deal with someone who wants to be doing what they do, or looks like it's the last thing in the world they want to be doing? The answer of course is obvious you want to work with others who bring a meaning-ful purpose to what they do. Your behavior is what shapes the impressions others have of you as well as their experiences when dealing with you. Repeat business is the product of consistently positive and constructive actions.

Buying most things means taking a leap of faith. Before your prospects or customers will buy from you they have to be confident the product or service you are selling is going to live up to their expectations. They look to you to be the guarantor that their expectations will be met. Thus before any sale can be made you must demonstrate that their confidence in you and whatever you're selling is warranted. Purchasing most things is really an exercise in perceived future value. Part of the decision to buy is based on our own interpretation of which of our needs the item being purchased will fill and another is how confident we are in the integrity of the product and the salesperson. Accordingly, when a product disappoints, this translates into disappointment in the salesperson. If not rectified quickly disappointment generally becomes resentment.

Perceptions are a powerful influencer. People make decisions everyday based on feelings and perceptions. What the mind perceives is usually what the customer believes. When the perception is positive a productive salesperson can take the next step. He or she can convert the customers positive perceptions into a belief in both themselves and the product or service being sold. It's because our feelings and perceptions are so personally a part of us that we feel so let down when they are proven wrong. We are seldom inclined to put them at risk again with the same salesperson.

What matters most in the long term is that you make sales with the customer's best interest at heart. The most powerful, effective and elusive selling tool you ever get to use is word of mouth validation. The only way you can build on this powerful and productive sales tool is one satisfied customer at a time. When it comes to opening doors and closing sales personal endorsements beat the heck out any marketing campaign I've ever seen. There's an old sales adage that's stood me in good stead over the years; under-sell and over-deliver. In other words to ensure a steady stream of satisfied customers, don't promise what you can't deliver. The road to failure is littered with the bones of salespeople who over hyped their sales presentations with rhetoric and promises that were never kept. One rule of successful selling that's been around since the first wheel was sold is; don't promise anything until you are absolutely positive you can deliver on the promise. The first casualties in a lot of sales presentations are truth and practicality.

Not all purchases require the buyers and sellers to work toward long-term mutually beneficial business relationships. When we're making one-time small ticket purchases, or when something of interest catches our eye we're going to make an impulse buy. If we think we need something badly enough no deliberate buying decision is required. In those cases, we're going to whip out our plastic and make a purchase regardless of the person selling the item. In situations like those , the people completing the transaction are simply facilitating the sale. It doesn't matter whether or not we develop rapport with them, or whether or not they have much product knowledge. They might even be personality challenged. It doesn't really matter. If our need for or fascination with the product is strong enough, we'll buy it. The value in these transactions is completely visible for you to see, touch, hear or smell. However, when purchasing some products or services the motive can be more significant and the role of the salesperson is more integral to the process. In those cases the salesperson becomes an important player in the buying decision.

Understanding your customer's likes, dislikes, needs, wants, and the way they like to conduct business is essential to the long term success of any sales practitioner who hopes to build on repeat business. Experience has taught me that you can be pretty safe in assuming that a large number if not all of your prospects and customers will share most if not all of the following common characteristics. First, they all want and need to feel accepted. Everyone wants to be part of a winning scenario. Your customers want to be convinced that any course of action they contemplate taking will result in positive recognition from others. That could include their boss, co-workers, family etc. Before they take action they want to be convinced the result of the actions they take will protect and enhance their self-esteem. The next one is really important because it speaks to the issue of your prospects or customers wanting to protect their own self-interest and feel good personally about the outcomes of decisions they make. We will always make our decisions with at least some consideration of "what's in it for me?" We want and need assurances that what we perceive to be our own unique needs and situations are being addressed, in a way that is custom tailored to us. Another commonality you can carve in stone is this. Every one of your prospects and customers will always prefer to talk about the things that are important to them. They might want your insight and advice and they might want to know whether or not the course of action you are recommending has worked for others, but in the end before they make a decision they will always bring it back to their own situation.

You may have the greatest sales presentation in the world. It might have sound and light effects that would rival a big budget Hollywood action thriller. That's terrific, but presentation aside, your sales effectiveness is going to come down to how easy it is for your prospects and customers to understand the key reasons to buy that are contained in the presentation. Feature those key points and don't muddy the water around them.

When all is said and done, it's all about the quality of your information and how you communicate it. Getting prospects and customers to make buying decisions is not about burying them in tons of generic information just to prove how knowledgeable you are. It's about providing them with concise information specific to their needs. The only information we retain is the information that's easy to remember. In the end it's not the quantity of information given that makes the difference it's the quality of the information retained that does.

Psychologists tell us we inevitably like, trust and believe others who we perceive to have some of the same outward interests, values and characteristics as us. Why should your prospects and customers be any different? I'm convinced this universal human tendency is a large factor in the burgeoning growth of golf courses as eighteen-hole-meeting rooms. Spending five hours sharing one common interest is bound to uncover others that can be talked about, laughed at or agonized over.

We all know from experience how quickly we can feel at ease with some people and uncomfortable with others. In the former case, you are very likely to be responding to your perceived commonality, in the latter to the lack-there-of. We all have an agenda, and we don't always share it. I mention this to help you understand, trying to think exactly like your prospects or customers will offer limited positive results. We can try to pre-suppose or try to anticipate responses and actions from others based on our way of thinking and doing but at best we are going to be successful a very small percentage of the time. I've been witness to more than a few salespeople talking themselves out of taking action because of the imagined responses they expect to get from prospects and customers. Selling is like a lot of contact sports, once you're in the game it's best to think less and do more. Once you've done your homework on a prospect or customer don't fall into paralysis by analysis. My advice is do less thinking about what might happen, and get on with doing what needs to be done to make it happen.

The Impact of personal quality on repeat business is significant. Repeat business is most often the result of the customer being satisfied with the performance of the product or service being sold and relating to and appreciating the qualities of the person doing the selling. It is my contention that mutually beneficial long-term relationships between buyers and sellers are driven by trust and performance. Trust is the foundation on which successful human enterprise rests. Trust and common values binds people together in shared causes. Throughout your professional life you will come to realize that without mutual trust, common goals and similar work ethics business relationships will not weather the storms that are bound to blow up from time to time.

Each of us I'm sure knows at least one person who on the surface would seem to have the schooling, the background and even the experience, to succeed as a professional sales practitioner, and yet doesn't. Failure in almost every case is at least partly due to a lack of commitment to professional quality. I don't mean the person in question is not a good person, who cares about his or her family and friends. I'm referring to the qualities they bring to their professional life. In a sales environment professional quality is shown in the way salespeople conduct their business and by the respect they show for their customers, colleagues and selves.

Here's my definition of professional quality. Quality is the result achieved by people who maintain a commitment to set and maintain personal and professional standards of performance high enough to consistently meet their own ideals and exceed the expectations of their customers. Some may ask; what's the motive to expend the effort and energy to develop and maintain a high level of professional quality? The answer is short and direct, customer loyalty. Everyone who jumps daily into the maelstrom of competitive business is aware of one irrefutable fact. In a world of ever-increasing, cut-throat competition loyal customers are becoming an endangered species. Hard to find and even more difficult to hold on to. One of the few ways to ensure any hope of customer loyalty is through professional quality. Which in this case means accepting the obligation to do what you say you're going to do, the way you said it would be done. It means placing a value on your word, making it count and looking at every customer problem as an opportunity to prove it.

Every sales professional with self respect who believes in themselves and the product or service they offer tries to satisfy their customers, but the ones that are a cut above the average go one step further, they are always working to convert satisfied into loyal customers. Developing a core group of loyal customers will make any sales territory more fun and more profitable to work. Loyal customer activists are the kind of customers who want to tell others about how good you are at what you do, and how pleased they are with both you and the product or service you represent. They will over time become your most vocal supporters.

In my experience customers can be loosely grouped into

three categories. The first group can be labeled performance buyers. Their buying impulse is triggered by their confidence in the performance of the product or service you're selling. The primary value they associate with any commodity is the worry free consistent performance of it. There is of course a limit to the premium these 'performance customers' will pay, but price is not the determining factor in their buying decisions. This category of customer represents the ideal customer profile for building long-term mutually profitable business relations.

The second category of customers can be labeled the personal service buyers. This group most highly values personal service and individual attention to detail. Again, price will be a factor in any buying decision but it won't be the primary one. This is another category of customer that sales-people can build solid working relationships with.

The third category can be labeled the bargain hunter buyers. For these customers the holy-grail is the lowest price. Price is the single determining factor in every purchase. Quality and service are always secondary to knocking off a nickel. You are not likely to build long term working relation-ships with these customers, because they are always on the hunt for the next bargain or lowest price. The term hunter is aptly applied to this group because they will kill your profit in their hunt for a bargain.

It is advantageous in the formative early stage of your selling career that you decide what category of customer you will target. Which category of customer fits best with the product or service that you are selling? At that point, you need to focus your efforts on filling the needs and meeting the expectations of the customers in that category. Bear in mind that we are living in an age of increasing specialization which means it is becoming more difficult and less profitable, to attempt to be all things to all customers.

Chapter Eight
Commitment vs. Involvement

Thinking all people who have jobs selling something
are equal to professional sales practitioners is like
finding a potato with a likeness of Jesus and
thinking you are witnessing the second coming.

Selling the product produced or the service provided has always been and will continue to be the driving force behind the success of every business. Nothing happens until some-one sells something to somebody is an old adage that continues to have currency in today's marketplace. Whether you own and operate a small business and take on the responsibility of generating sales or you hold a management position in a sales department or you are part of a team of professional sales practitioners you have one thing in common. Increased market share and revenue will be determined by making more sales to existing customers and new sales to prospective customers. A macro view of today's increasingly global-markets shows they offer both great opportunities and increased challenges to the people charged with the responsibility of getting goods sold. Similarly a micro view uncovers the irrefutable fact that regardless of what business sector you operate in, you are subject to living and working amidst an ever–expanding and ever–changing economy. The demand for growth in sales revenue and market share while working in often-chaotic conditions brought about by ever shifting customer priorities and demands means a dynamic response in both the way you think and the actions you take is called for. It means you are going to have to find ways to stay abreast of the pace of change even if that means having to take on the challenge of tossing out some time-tested ways of doing things or re-inventing how they're done. Salespeople are the front line troops of any organization. You are the window through which customer's see your organization. For that reason alone salespeople and those responsible for their actions must be flexible enough to adapt to change and courageous enough to cause some of their own.

It's not new ideas and new ways of doing things that should scare anyone. It's the results of old ideas and outdated ways of doing things that should. Sometimes we need to remind ourselves that every new beginning comes from some other beginnings end. The expansion of sales revenue and existing market share and branching out into new sectors to create new additional market share can only be accomplished by people using new creative selling methods in equally creative new ways. In any case outselling the competition remains the name of the game. For the overly zealous exponents of change at any cost let me throw in a note of caution here. The idea of changing your way of playing the game to take full advantage of the change in the rules and the new parameters established by those playing against you does not include radically altering the way you build your customer relationships. Recent studies validate and reinforce the idea that people want to buy goods and services from salespeople with whom they share common values and disciplines and,

- are reliable and have integrity
- are pleasant to deal with and make them feel comfortable
- can be trusted with personal or confidential information
- keep them informed with topical and concise information
- are willing partners in problem solving

- can be counted on to put the needs of the customer before the need for a sale

Today we have entire business sectors that once ignored the need to sell their product or service embracing the need for more direct sales to their customers with a zeal and passion reserved for the newly converted. There is hardly a product or service provider anywhere who doesn't understand that the surest way to grow their business is to get out and make some sales. The banking, medical, dental and accounting sectors are good examples of businesses and professions that at one time thought themselves immune to the need to generate new revenues through increased sales. They now consider selling an integral part of their business and operating plans they recognize and acknowledge the importance of being able to sell to their customers. They understand the only way to expand their revenue is through sales of additional products or services. You can hardly attend a party today without some dentist selling you on the wonders of bleaching your teeth or an eye doctor extolling the virtues of laser eye surgery. They have all come to understand that failure to sell means failure to grow. Inability to sell their services to existing and potential customers means risking being cast aside in favor of competitors who can.

It's your commitment that counts. Salespeople are made not born! Selling is part science, part art, part fun and a whole lot of hard work. Unfortunately hard work alone doesn't guarantee equality of results. It only guarantees equality of opportunity. Let me lay one myth to rest right away. Successful sales professionals are not born. They are made and they are made from the inside out. Like any other professional, sales practitioners have to learn and apply skills that are specific to the job they do. Through practice and repletion these skills become deeply ingrained and second nature to every successful salesperson. Anyone who has ever been consistently successful selling anything knows their results rise and fall on how well they are able to apply their skills. The difference between being involved and being committed is like the ham and eggs you might have had for breakfast. In that case the chicken was involved but the pig was totally committed. The workplace is full of people who are involved but lack commitment. How many people do you think get up every day without any interest in or excitement for the job they do. There are legions of people shuffling through their morning rituals already bored with the thought of another day of doing what they do even before they start doing it. They go to work and go through the motions of working and produce acceptable results. Their involvement begins when they arrive at work but their commitment was lost a long time ago. This workforce of bored workers toiling in non-challenging jobs makes up a large percentage of the workforce in any workplace anywhere at anytime. They go to work for one common reason, financial necessity.

They aren't able to find and in most cases aren't looking for any intrinsic satisfaction in what they do, or how they do it. In many jobs the efforts of the people doing them never really seems to have a measurable impact on the fortunes of the organization or the department they are part of. Let's face it in some cases some jobs are just plain boring. There is dignity in all work, but one of the intrinsic realities in the work world is, some jobs are simply more interesting and personally satisfying than others.

I consider sales professionals to be among the fortunate people in the work place. They work in jobs that in many ways are some of the most interesting, challenging and personally rewarding anyone could have. But, those jobs come with the proviso that only the people willing to make a commitment to doing them well will prosper. Salespeople don't last long just being involved. They like our friend the pig in our example have to be totally committed to what they do and how they do it, if they hope to have a long and prosperous career. Salespeople unlike most others work in an environment that offers almost continuous ongoing challenges. They also have the advantage and sometimes disadvantage of seeing the results of their efforts measured as they go. They get to see firsthand the impact of their efforts. This instant gratification and validation of their efforts, or lack there of, is of course a classic example of the good news bad news scenario at work. Salespeople more so than most, need a steady stream of positive feedback to fuel their determination. When all is well in the kingdom the determination to do more is fed. When all is not so well that same determination can begin to wane.

I've always figured that even on the worst of days working at something you want to do, enjoy doing and are committed to doing well has to beat the heck out of doing something you have to do, but don't really want to be doing. In my experience, sales practitioners who enjoy long and rewarding careers always find a way to get enjoyment out of what they do, while doing it. It's another positive linear relationship. They like what they do, so they make the effort to become better at doing it. Then, the better at it they get the more they like doing it.

It becomes a well-defined blueprint for success. The better at it they get the more refined their selling smarts become and the more effectively they are able to use their skills. Selling smarts are hard to quantify or define. First off, having selling smarts is not the same as being smart, at least not in the conventional sense of the word. This is in no way meant to denigrate the intelligence of sales people. Society for the most part does however, tend to mistake knowledge for wisdom and education for intelligence. Most of us have a tendency to measure a person's level of intelligence by the number of degrees they hold. Even though Albert Einstein who most would consider the pre-eminent thinker of the modern age is quoted as saying, he was happy to have completed his formal education so that he could get on with the business of learning. A good formal education does not always make for good selling smarts.

Top sales professionals have an affinity for being able to blend together a mix of intelligence, street smarts and selling smarts. My definitions for each are as follows; intelligence is knowing the answer or where to look for it, street smarts is the ability to reason something through to a logical and workable solution and selling smarts is the ability to apply selling skills in consistently productive ways. A couple of key components of selling smarts are. First knowing how to communicate with people as they are, not as you would like them to be. Second, being able to think creatively while acting pragmatically. Selling smarts may not be what you would use to split the atom, but they're pretty handy when you're trying to bring people, ideas and products or services together.

Chapter Nine
Managing Anxiety and Rejection

*No one can make you feel inferior
without your consent.*

At the outset of a career in professional sales, unless you figure out ways to manage the twin evils of prospecting anxiety and fear of rejection the price you pay for success will be much higher than it need be or should be. Prospecting anxiety and fear of rejection are the two factors most responsible for the destruction of potentially productive selling careers since the first sales team was assembled to sell the new fangled wheel to other cave dwellers. They are the two most prevalent and potentially damaging psychological barriers faced by professional salespeople. They can in the extreme provoke enough anxiety and phobia to drive potentially good salespeople to give up on themselves and seek other means of earning their income. In less extreme cases they can subtly affect your selling performance by causing you to shy away from the challenge of going after lucrative new business.

There is no way to sugar coat the reality that in order to prosper every sales professional must put themselves on the line and face the possibility of having themselves and their ideas, products or services rejected. Anxiety and fear of rejection become debilitating problems only when you let yourself succumb to the feelings that accompany them. Those feelings show up as stress, tension, apprehension, worry and a growing sense of personal inadequacy and a lessening of self-confidence. Since our feelings fuel our attitude, thoughts, ideas and actions you can see how destructive the impact of negative anxiety can be.

Every professional sales practitioner must find a consistently workable way to manage the challenge of over-coming anxiety and rejection before they can move forward and reach an above average level of performance and income. Notice I said manage not overcome. I don't believe there is any way to completely overcome the anxiety and fear of rejection that is part and parcel to a selling career. In fact and this might surprise you, I think a little well managed anxiety can be a good thing. It can heighten your senses and give you the little adrenaline boost you might need from time to time. One of the world's great actors Sir Lawrence Olivier was once asked late in his career if he still got stage fright. He replied; "yes and when I don't I'll know it's time to quit". He went on to explain that he didn't waste energy trying to completely overcome his anxiety but instead used the energy created by it to improve his performance. He put it this way; "I never try to get rid of the butterflies in my stomach, I just work at getting them to fly in formation".

If you began reading this chapter in the hope that some-where in it you'd find the definitive answer to the problem of prospecting anxiety and fear of rejection, let me spare you some time and effort, move on to the next chapter. If I had the answer rest assured I would share it with you. The bare bones truth is, there isn't one. I can however offer you some solace by suggesting that in the pages to follow you just might find your way to get your butterflies to fly in formation.

Prospecting anxiety is something encountered by almost every sales professional at some time during their career. Just do it, is an admirable rallying cry, easier said than done. Sales professionals face a deceptively simple in theory but complex in practice challenge everyday. It comes with varying degrees of difficulty depending on their state of mind. They face the daunting challenge of jumping out of bed every morning and as a sales manager I once worked for succinctly put it; going out and selling their faces off.

The initiative required to put in a productive selling day has little to do with your capabilities as a salesperson. In this case it isn't what you know, but how you feel that will make or break your day.

When your ball of string is unraveling as it should, you're likely to be ready, willing and able to face the demands of the day. Chances are you're ready to face the day with vigor and self-assured determination.   When you're on a roll there aren't enough hours in the day. The sales tree is ripe for the picking and you're looking to fill your basket. It's like you're locked onto autopilot, moving in a straight line from one good result to the next. You have an inner sense of well-being that makes you move a little quicker and walk a little taller. Ah, life is good. I've been there I know what it's like to feel invincible. You're not just making the sales you're working on but it seems like others that you had given up on suddenly spring back to life. One incident in support of what I'm talking about occurred when I had worked with a prospect for over six months on a sale that would generate substantial commission dollars to me, only to see it go to a competitor. I decided to try to keep my hat in the ring for the future by convincing the buyer to use me as her secondary supplier. It was over three months later when during a time when I was on a sales roll that I received a call from this prospect asking me if I was in a position to step in and fill the order. It seems that my competitor had been having shipping and quality problems from the get go. Finally in frustration the buyer turned to me to help solve the problem. Sure I had worked hard on the project during the time I was competing for it and I had made the effort to maintain a relationship with the prospect even though near term sales didn't seem to be in the cards, but I would be lying if I said I hadn't parked the prospect in my 'one day something might develop' file.

Rarely however, can we walk the beach without getting the occasional grain of sand in our shoe. Nothing lasts forever. An admonition that seems particularly appropriate to the ups and downs of professional sales. The flip side of riding the selling wave is to find yourself being sucked down by the undertow of a sales slump. It's when your world is unraveling instead of unfolding that you find yourself staring into the unblinking eye of the sales worlds scariest Cyclops, prospecting anxiety.

Any bout of prospecting anxiety can turn the demands of selling your product or service into a monster you would much rather run from than fight with. Without the right mindset and the ability to tap into your performance strengths your anxiety can turn your thoughts inward to the point where self-preservation not personal productivity becomes the order of the day. If left unabated prospecting anxiety carries with it the very real possibility of discouraging salespeople to the point where they would rather give in to failure than have to face another day of it.

Anxiety of course is most prevalent among newly minted salespeople. It begins for some even as they wrestle with the decision of whether or not a career in professional sales is for them. For others, who have made a decision to try to become proficient salespeople, it's even more damaging. Their anxiety can cause them to question the very validity of their new selling career. A career in professional sales differs in one significant aspect from most others. The majority of people who find themselves trying to make it in the world of professional sales, never start out with selling as their number one career choice. A lot are draftees not volunteers. Those for whom selling is a second or third choice or even the career court of last resort find the demands of professional sales puzzling, daunting and even demeaning. The initial challenge for a lot of those people is to overcome their own negative perceptions about being labeled a sales-person. Without a full appreciation of the differences between hucksterism and professional selling they worry about what some of their peers may think about them. First off let's consider this, a lot of us wouldn't worry so much about what others think of us, if we really knew how seldom they did. People who suffer salesperson inferiority always seem to forget the undeniable fact that most people in everyday life are called on to make sales. The selling they do might not be

the kind we associate with making a living doing it b
doesn't alter the fact that people are always trying to mak
sales in the most unlikely selling situations.

Teachers better be able to sell the importance of learning
and the benefits of education. Newspapers sell you on the
idea that there's is the best source for news. You need to sell
yourself on the benefits of losing weight or quitting smoking
before you can have success doing either. Your kids are
selling you on the advantages of having a car of their own. I
can categorically state that from cradle to grave almost
everyone you interact with is selling you something in some
way at least some of the time. We just have other names for
it, like, being advised, choosing options, considering
alternatives and making informed decisions. But in the final
analysis it's selling.

A good selling environment is rich in enthusiasm,
motivating influences and resonates with positive thoughts
and ideas. For that reason you seldom see selling skills
trainers spend too much time or put to much emphasis on
perceived negatives like prospecting anxiety. In most courses
for instance, more time is devoted to overcoming buyer
resistance and ways of closing the sale. When prospecting
anxiety is dealt with at all it's usually with an eye to offering
ways to get around it, not address the likely causes of it. Some
time tested solutions to the problem are offered. Consider
each no as getting you closer to a yes. Divide the
commissions earned from your sales by the number of sales
calls you make and put a value on each. Cast a wide net and
you're bound to catch some fish. I've used those and other
ways to help motivate myself and get around the anxiety I
encountered from time to time.

Every organization works hard to uncover and recruit
people they think will make productive salespeople. Part of
the reason for skirting the issue of prospecting anxiety in
company sales training seminars is the fear that it will raise
negative issues and quite frankly undermine the confidence
of new sales recruits. I've written enough sales training
manuals and programs to know most clients want a sunshine

lollipops and roses training course. I've been told by countless clients; "make sure you focus on the positives and eliminate the negatives". "We want our training courses to focus on teaching easy to learn and easy to apply techniques for getting from opening the door to closing the sale". Neophyte salespeople are taught proven and practical ways to identify customer needs, create prospect interest, overcome any and all objection and close the sale. Rarely if ever are they taught how to manage their own prospecting anxiety.

Of course when dealing with the prospecting anxiety dilemma some salespeople are luckier than others. You may already have built up such a substantial base of customers that generating any more new business would just put a strain on the production capabilities of your company. Maybe you generate so much income from existing customers that any new commissions earned will only put you into a new tax bracket. Perhaps the product or service is in such demand that people throw their doors open and thank you for taking the time to see them and for giving them the opportunity to buy what you're selling. Now lets step out of the twilight zone and get back to reality. Almost anything that can be bought needs to be sold, before anyone decides to buy it.

The importance of helping salespeople identify and deal with the root problem of prospecting anxiety is in direct proportion to the how often it is likely to be encountered. Its impact on salespeople often varies according to the type of product or service being sold. Salespeople who are charged with the responsibility of generating a consistent flow of new selling leads encounter it most. This would include for example people in the real estate, insurance, and financial planning sectors. Regardless of what you sell the chances are pretty good you're going to have to make some calls on prospects to try to generate additional business.

Learning how to manage your prospecting anxiety is as important to salespeople as learning how to take off and land their plane is to pilots. I doubt if we'd have many successful pilots if we sent them to flight schools that only taught them how to fly a plane while ignoring the take off and landing parts of the process. Anyone familiar with piloting a plane will tell you all the work is in getting it off the ground and returning safely to it. It's relatively easy to fly once you're in the air. As one pilot friend put it; flying the plane is ninety percent boring and ten percent sweaty palms. Prospecting anxiety is not just a challenge faced exclusively by people new to the rigors of selling. I've worked with highly successful experienced salespeople who for no apparent reason find themselves mired in prolonged sales slumps. Once we sit down and analyze their situation the cause of the slump becomes apparent and it can almost always be traced back to prospecting anxiety. It usually happens after someone has been on a sales roll for a while. They have been generating their business from established customer referrals, not having to make any calls to prospects to try to initiate new selling opportunities. But nothing ever lasts forever and one day the volume of referrals goes down and the need to make sales calls goes up and sometimes with the need comes the anxiety.

Anyone who has ever made their living selling has suffered prospecting anxiety to some degree at some time. The difference between those who succeed in spite of it, and those who fail by succumbing to it, is pretty simple. The salespeople who succeed know how to reach down and tap into their reserves of performance qualities and use them to generate the determination to take whatever actions are needed to deal with and overcome their anxiety.

Those who fail waste their time hoping that somehow their prospecting anxiety will just magically get up and go away, instead of instituting the actions necessary to drive it away. There's a real irony to it because prospecting anxiety keeps you from being active and making things happen. At the same time, sales professionals understand that it's activity, that makes things happen and drives away prospecting anxiety.

There are a number of simple everyday factors that can and do contribute to prospecting anxiety. Some are more applicable to the less experienced salespeople among us. Finding a way to deal constructively with the variables encountered in prospecting and selling situations can be particularly challenging for people who are used to being in control of what they are doing and generate results by following a set pattern of actions. Do this to get this. If you've spent most or all of your time at a job or career where almost everything you did was in your control and you knew that if you did a certain thing in a certain way the results would seldom vary, finding yourself in a sales driven environment prospecting for new customers can be pretty challenging.

Most selling situations could be described as controlled chaos. There is no formula to follow that guarantees success. Sales success is achieved most often through a pattern of probabilities. You do your best to do what you have to, to create consistently productive selling opportunities and then when all is said and done you hope for the best. If there was one proven way to make sales and never miss it would be easy, but it's not, because the one factor constant in every sales situation is, there is no one best way of doing and no fool proof way to guarantee getting it done.

Salespeople understand that even the best among them, are caught in a numbers game. You have to find a way to create consistent sales opportunities in order to generate consistent sales. The only thing that differs is the sales opportunity to sales result ratio. When you are able to learn and apply productive selling skills your sales call to sales closed ratio improves. I've witnessed top producing sales people earn high incomes from relatively few sales opportunities because of their ability to convert a higher than average number of their opportunities into sales, while others generate more opportunities but end up with fewer sales because of some flaw in their selling technique.

To me, one of the key differences in the results is that successful salespeople expect to make the sale. They have a passion for what they are doing and they exhibit a calm self-confidence going into every sales opportunity. They visualize the expected results in terms of a positive return on their time and effort. They have learned how to exhibit their confidence in a way that increases the customer's comfort level and makes it easier for them to take action and complete the sale. On the other hand, those who struggle with their confidence are most likely to visualize negative consequences to their actions, if they visualize at all. They expect to fail and are almost always surprised when they make a sale. They condition themselves to accept failure and in so doing they also condition themselves to fail. Failure for them becomes a self–fulfilling prophecy.

Fear of rejection is constant in any situation where other people hold sway over the yes's or no's. You can make a terrific sales presentation to one customer and get the positive response you hoped for, then repeat the presentation almost verbatim to the next and be rejected. When it comes to everyday fears, our fear of being rejected ranks at or near the top of most lists. In fact psychologists suggest fear of rejection beats out a whole litany of other more commonly thought of fears such as, fear of snakes, fear of public speaking or fear of having your in-laws move in with you.

We aren't just talking about rejection in a sales situation I mean the number one fear of people in any walk of life is the fear of being rejected. So it figures that the number one need all of us have is the need for acceptance. I can think of very few careers that match that of a professional sales practitioner in terms of potential rejection. Every time a sales-person puts him or herself on the line in a prospecting or selling situation they are putting themselves at risk of being rejected.

When your income is largely based on the sales you produce, how well you are able to deal with and manage the potentially damaging impact of rejection and the anxiety it produces will go a long way to determining the level of your income. Contrary to the positive rhetoric found in some sales training courses no one ever learns to like it or ever completely learns to ignore it. The truth is rejection hurts. I was told from day one in my sales career to remember that what people were rejecting was my product or service and not me personally. Comforting words, but they still didn't ease the sting of being rejected and losing a sale. The only consistently way I found to deal positively with the negativity of rejection was to always be working to create enough sales opportunities so that any one situation alone did not hold the potential to do significant damage to my income or psyche. In spite of my best efforts to manage rejection it would still occasionally get me down. When it did, I got back on track by focusing on the realization that facing rejection was the price I had to pay to be successful in my job.

In over thirty years of trying to sell something to somebody, I still feel good when whatever I'm selling is accepted and bad when it isn't. I do take it personally. Writing books is a far cry from the daily challenge of working a sales territory, but it still contains an element of selling and includes the risk of rejection. In order to be judged a success, the books I write must be bought by people and enjoyed by the people buying them. In fact for authors rejection can be a double-edged sword. Whenever I write a book my first hope is that people will buy it, so that my efforts haven't been wasted, but of equal importance is that they enjoy and get something out of the book. That's the real reason any writer writes. The rejection of being turned down for instance by a book store buyer who doesn't want to carry my book, is nothing compared to the impact of being rejected by meeting someone who bought my book and didn't enjoy reading it. On the other hand I never get tired of being complimented by others who buy the book and tell me how much they enjoyed it or learned from it.

When you're a salesperson and you put yourself on the line everyday and find yourself in situations where people either accept or reject what you have to offer, you are wasting your time trying to find the magic bean that will help you overcome the effects of rejection. I say this because the more you dwell on the impact of rejection the greater the impact is. My advice is to accept the reality of the situation and the reality is that a certain amount of rejection goes with the job. There's always a price to pay for whatever we are trying to accomplish in any career, the price salespeople pay is rejection. Anytime you exchange ideas and information with someone, which of course is a part of what making a sales presentation is, it gives the person you are making the presentation to, the option to agree or disagree. When they agree, you feel accepted when they disagree you feel rejected. One way then to cut down on rejection and increase acceptance is to improve your ability to communicate your message. One other way that I found helped me to keep rejection in perspective was to tell myself that only by creating opportunities to be rejected would I put myself in a position to make sales. The more rejection I risked the more sales I would be rewarded with. When you take action it either works or it doesn't. But one thing we know for sure is if fear of rejection keeps you from taking any action, you sure as heck aren't going to accomplish anything.

Fear of rejection is constant in our lives and it first introduces itself to most of us during our adolescence and at very inopportune times. My earliest recollection of the impact of fear of rejection can best be described to you by relating the following scenarios. Some of the male readership of this book might remember as I do the indelible imprint left on impressionable and insecure psyches when the ritual of picking players for teams took place. Standing lined up with the rest of the hopefuls waiting to be picked for the team, and finally being chosen last, right after the guy with the cast on his broken arm.

If that recollection of rejection doesn't make you shudder, try this one, it too might stir a few memories. It's the once a month junior high school dance. You've made a critical error in judgment and confided in a few friends your interest in one particular member of the opposite gender. You now find yourself after being taunted by your sensitive and caring brothers in arms, taking that long lonely walk across the gymnasium floor to ask the apple of your eye for a dance. If you've ever been through it you will remember ambling awkwardly across the floor praying desperately to any God who might be listening that she wouldn't reject you and turn you down. Once you've faced up to that possibility of rejection, everything else in life is easy.

Every sales skills training course makes every effort to address the issue of sales presentation rejection and provide participants with ideas on how to manage or overcome it. The training professionals who conduct the courses try to provide ways to lessen the impact of rejection because they know rejection hurts. They also know in the beginning you will probably take it too personally and they know that if you don't adjust to it your career in sales will be short lived. Lets expose one very basic truth here, rejection is painful and we do take it personally. Why, because we almost always measure our self-worth by what we accomplish at the job we do. We too often measure our success as people on the basis of how readily our ideas and actions are accepted by everyone around us. In every professional sales environment I've ever been part of success is ultimately measured solely in terms of the results of the salesperson's selling efforts. The real danger lies in relinquishing your emotional well-being, and letting others control it by basing your self-worth solely on their acceptance or rejection of you, your opinions, ideals, values and ideas. Professional sales practitioners more so than most others have to constantly be vigilant about the dangers of basing their self-worth solely on the results they generate in their jobs.

When we are unable to separate who we are from what we do, we risk buying a ticket to ride a life long emotional roller coaster whose ups and downs are controlled by everyone and everything but us. The temptation to judge ourselves solely by what we accomplish starts in our formative years. We are taught from an early age that failure brings rejection and rejection results in failure. No wonder we such have an unhealthy respect for it and fear of it. The fear of rejection can build impenetrable walls around us because it will eventually rob us of hope and hope is what drives us toward our goals and helps us find the courage to take the actions needed to reach them. The early stage of a selling career is when the slap of rejection stings the most. It has greater negative impact and hurts more than it should because you feel pressured to generate immediate results and because of that you tend to place way too much importance on each sales opportunity that results from your prospecting activities. Those of us who have been through it, can attest that at the beginning of our careers it seemed like every proposal or sales presentation we made carried with it the potential to make or break us. When you're starting out, each selling opportunity is magnified in importance. Each one can be intimidating because so much rides on the outcome. Each opportunity takes on a life of its' own. Depending on the results each one holds the power to lift your emotions and make you feel more confident or knock you down and make you question your selling ability.

I can tell you not to take sales presentation rejection personally, that it's just part of the selling game you've chosen to play, but that isn't going to make it hurt any less or the pain go away any sooner. I can however, offer you this thought; the magnitude of any single sales presentation you make, is directly proportional to the number you are making. Over time as you build your prospect and customer base and you begin generating more sales presentation opportunities each will be seen in a more realistic perspective. Experience will help you put your sales presentation opportunities into the proper perspective and you will realize they are opportunities to generate sales and earn income, not life and death struggles.

Don't let fear of rejection turn you into an avoider. Avoidence is the career destroyer and life influencer that can result from an inability to find a way to deal constructively with the impact of rejection. If you don't find a way to accept rejection as part of the selling game, cope with it and find a way to lessen its' impact on you, the fear of being rejected will almost certainly result in your becoming an avoider. An avoider is someone who will go to great lengths to avoid putting themselves into any situation where they might be confronted by rejection. They see no upside in challenging themselves. To do so would mean placing themselves and their egos in jeopardy. Their operating credo becomes if I don't play to win, I can't lose. They seek to avoid the pressure and possible rejection that achievers face by simply giving up and settling for a less demanding job and an average lifestyle. Average isn't something anyone should ever strive for.

Find something that doesn't take too much effort and doesn't demand too much risk taking and just become productive enough to fit in and get by, becomes their mantra. How they think and what they do is negatively influenced by one overriding thought, when I give up and decide not to play my chances of losing or being rejected disappear. My ego won't be bruised and my fear of failure will go away. If I just do enough to get by, I won't face the constant pressure that is part and parcel to excelling at whatever I choose to do. They become content to just be average. What we need to remind ourselves of once in a while is this; average isn't something anyone ever strives for, but it is something too many people end up settling for.

The cold hard fact is the world we live and work in is inhabited by countless numbers of avoiders. People who have sold out their dream and quit on themselves. People who decide for them the race to succeed, to move forward, and to win is too tough. Avoiders never arrive at a destination of choice they drift to wherever life takes them. Avoiders pay a hidden and heavy price for giving up and giving in, because they can only attain their objective of competitive avoidance by standing aside and watching others move forward.

There is a price to be paid for giving up and giving in. If becoming an avoider doesn't appeal to you then you're going to have to confront your fear of rejection and find a way to manage it. One way to put it into perspective is to take a hard look at the price you will pay for giving in to it. We know the best way to avoid rejection is to take no actions. We also know the only way to reach our goals and objectives is by taking constructive actions. Quite a dilemma isn't it? One way to solve it is to stop and think about the consequences that result from our hesitancy or unwillingness to take action. If we're unwilling to place ourselves in the path of possible rejection do the possible consequences outweigh the potential return.

We need to think about whether our concerns are justified or just the result of blind unreasonable fears that hold us hostage. Successful sales practitioners are the first to understand the only way to create sales potential is by being active and making things happen. They understand there are concrete reasons why some prospects or customers may reject their ideas, products or services, and that those reasons may not be able to be dealt with or overcome. They've learned not to spend their time and emotional energy flogging a dead horse. Once they've done their best with the circumstances presented to them, they accept what is and move on. They spend their time dealing with the reality of what is, and don't waste valuable time clinging to loss causes.

Sometimes we fail because we become so paralyzed by the fear of what might be, we become unable to work toward the potential of what could be. Imagined fears are formless, elusive and very difficult to deal with, trying to fight them is like trying to capture a fistful of fog. No matter how difficult it may be, the best way to set aside our imagined fears of rejection and overcome the accompanying inertia caused by them, is to make a commitment to ourselves to take the actions necessary to put ourselves into situations that will generate responses either positive or negative. Only then can we turn our imagined fears into real situations and scenarios that we can deal with. Giving in to fear of rejection robs sales practitioners of the opportunity to maximize their potential. Letting fear restrict your actions is a far greater risk to your success than any potential negative consequences resulting from any actions you might take.

Chapter Ten
Find Your Self-Motivation

When you put a small value on yourself,
you can be pretty sure no on is going to raise it.

The performance qualities you will rely on most to manage anxiety and rejection will be self-motivation and self-confidence. There is just no way you can be motivated by yourself or someone else to take on the challenge of facing the possibility of rejection with the frequency that it occurs in professional sales, until you have confidence that you know what you are doing. If you don't believe in yourself and your abilities and aren't convinced you possess the tools and skills to do the job and you aren't sure what you are doing will benefit your customers, trying to find the will and determination to overcome prospecting anxiety and fear of rejection will be impossible. .

The only motivation that will consistently generate enough confidence to take on and overcome your fear of rejection and the accompanying prospecting anxiety has to be founded on the belief that you possess the tools and the skills to use them. The ensuing confidence will instill the determination you need to get out and put them to work productively. In other words you're not likely to be anxious to climb on your horse and gallop into the fight without knowing a thing or two about riding and fighting. When my customers call and ask me to do motivational talks for their employees. I tell them flat out that I can and will do a motivating talk, one that will get their people excited about getting out and using their knowledge and skills more often. But, if they aren't providing their people with the tools to do the job and teaching them how to use them effectively, the talk will only result in increased activity and increased frustration because they are bound to generate the same old results.

The real key to lasting motivation is to find ways to motivate yourself. The cornerstone that all motivation is built on whether someone else is trying to motivate you or you're trying to motivate yourself is your own self-confidence. Only when you are confident you possess the tools and skills to be effective will you have the confidence to look ahead to the results of putting them to work for you. That's when you can become motivated, because the bottom line on what you are being motivated by, is your own expectation of success. A good motivator is someone who can help you become self-motivated. Outside motivation can never be anything other than a quick positive shot in the arm that will give you a lift, but only for a short time. Self-motivation is long lasting, it's what pushes us to learn new skills and then look for ways to apply our new skills to increase our productivity.

I've often been asked to conduct programs to get failing or underachieving salespeople back on track. In this case the people involved are usually well qualified to do the job. They have extensive product knowledge and they possess good selling skills. They are just not motivated to want to be successful. The customers who hire me to work with these people have the best of intentions. They want to help their people to prosper and be successful. They want them to be happy and know the satisfaction of being recognized for their accomplishments. The trouble is, everyone around these unmotivated people is doing the wanting for them. Nothing will change until the unmotivated find their own motivation. An unmotivated salesperson never sees any urgency to make things happen. They are content to just do what it takes to get by. They set low performance standards for themselves and achieve correspondingly low results. To these people making more sales calls just means uncovering more potential problems to be dealt with, not opportunities to take advantage of.

An unmotivated salesperson who never finds their own self-generated motivation will over time develop a lethargic way of doing things. They begin to show a distinct disinterest in what needs to be done, and a cynical attitude about the people around them. These are most definitely not the type of characteristics or attributes needed for a successful career in professional sales. If you're intent on raising the level of your productivity ask yourself the following questions.

1. Are you confident that you possess the knowledge and skills needed to be successful in most selling situations?
2. If you do, are you self-motivated enough to want to put your knowledge and skills to use, to make yourself successful? If you answered yes to both questions I have one more for you.
3. Do you have in writing a list of goals and objectives that you are motivated to achieve?

Think of motivation as raw energy. In order to get the maximum benefit from that energy you need to put it to work as an energizing force. You need to connect your motivational energy to a series of interim objectives. Your interim objectives are the wires your motivational energy travels though to get you to your long-term goals.

The world of professional sales is, in many ways a harsh and demanding landscape. It is one that demands personal accountability. Salespeople don't work in a vacuum. Most have support teams behind them from administration to operations to management to help them achieve their productivity goals and make their jobs easier. However, when the rubber hits the road, it is the salesperson you who is accountable for the sales they do or don't make. The salespeople who prosper most are the ones who understand one undeniable fact. They are the ones their customers are most likely to hold personally accountable for the performance of the product or service they sell. They also know that an unyielding commitment to accept responsibility for what they have control over is the mark of a true professional.

If it is to be, it is up to me. Personal accountability means you don't whine about what 'coulda been, or shoulda been' or 'mighta been'. Instead, it means you accept the message found in the old adage, 'you reap what you sow'. Other than some occasional random occurrences, more often than not we create our own circumstances. The circumstances and situations we inevitably find ourselves in, are the direct result of actions we willingly choose to take or not take. Personal accountability for the results of your thoughts and actions is consistent with personal achievement. You have two options in life. Take control of your life through personal accountability, or accept no personal accountability and let others chart the course of your life. When you choose the latter course, you must also be prepared to relinquish control over the level of your achievements.

Don't get in the habit of victimizing yourself. Personal accountability is the direct link between your thoughts, your actions and the outcomes. People who struggle seldom if ever fully understand the downside of not accepting accountability for their thoughts and actions. The inevitable temptation to see and think of themselves as victims, becomes the downside. They feel not only victimized by people, but generally, by all that surrounds them. When the company advertising isn't bringing in as many prospects as they think it should, or when the marketing brochures aren't having the impact they think they should, then they of course are the victims of someone else's ineptitude. It's always the people around them, but never themselves who are too stupid to understand the situation. When customers aren't responding it's the people behind the quality of the service or the product, or the system or the process who are all conspiring to create difficulties for them.

Those who try to deflect accountability are quick to become negative and defensive under stress. They attribute their failings to everyone and everything but themselves. Anyone intent on proceeding through life in this manner, upset and angry and believing the failings of others are directly responsible for their under-achieving is bound to experience failure first-hand. The only way to stop victimizing yourself is to accept accountability for the thoughts that precede your actions. Your ineffective actions are the direct result and are fed by the negativity of your thoughts. If you persist in the belief that you are being held back from attaining your goals because 'they' just won't listen, or 'they' just don't get it, you're doomed to failure.

Nothing is going to change until you are ready to accept accountability for finding new and more constructive ways of thinking about and dealing with the people and things around you. The proof is always in the results. If you're always so right and so smart then why aren't you generating the results that you want? Stop looking in the wrong places and at the wrong people for the answers to your problems. It's time to look within yourself. The most destructive mode of thinking for any salesperson is to convince yourself that you and you alone have all the right answers. That you are always right, no matter what. Anyone with this egocentric type of attitude is on the fast track to customer rejection and personal failure. This self-righteous thinking leads to believing that you are one of the chosen smart ones and all others are the unfortunately ignorant. In any problem-solving situation you are inexorably right and they are inarguably wrong. Those who don't understand your point of view or share your opinion are at best misinformed and at worst just plain stupid. At first glance because of an often-assertive demeanor and attitude these self-victimizing people can actually appear to be very self-confident. The opposite in fact, holds true. What at fist appears to be self-confidence is really self-righteous aggression. It's their self-defense mechanism. They use it to protect them from having to face up to the failures we all sometimes encounter. In addition it allows them to avoid accountability for creating negative situations and the resulting set backs that follow.

Almost without exception we create the situations we find ourselves in and we are the ones responsible for the emotions we feel because of those situations. When we too often find ourselves mired in negative and self-defeating situations we need to take action to change the way we think and the things we do. The whole process of change for the better can begin only when we accept our role in the process that's holding us back. Then we have to make ourselves accountable for improving it. It's only then that we can give ourselves the freedom to take the required actions and make the required changes that will result in real and lasting change.

There is a good news upside to all of this. When you acknowledge that the solutions to your problems are controlled and driven by you, you can in a remarkably short time begin your journey from where you are to where you want to be. You can begin by getting away from the victimizing pattern of thinking 'Why did this happen to me?' or "Why are they doing this to me? That kind of thinking only leads you to discount your involvement. You need to accept your involvement before you can take steps to change it.

To make meaningful changes and stick with them, you need to focus your thoughts on what is now and what lies ahead, not what was then and what you've left behind. One way to make sure you don't fall into the trap of victimizing yourself is to ask yourself the following questions and take a hard look at your answers.

- What things have I done that I had personal control over that have contributed to the situations I find myself in?
- What can I without the help of others do to improve those situations?
- What specific negative circumstances in my life could be improved by positive thoughts, attitudes, behaviors and actions?
- What specific thoughts, behaviors and actions should I concentrate on?

- What attitudes, behaviors and actions contribute most to my success?

After you take an honest objective look at your answers, it should become clear to you that you are singly responsible for the results you are achieving. Compare closely what attitudes and actions have contributed most to your successes and failures. Part of maximizing your effectiveness is being able to understand when you're on the right path or have strayed into the bush. This type of analysis when done consistently will help you determine the behaviors and actions you should be focusing on to enable you to reach your goals.

Chapter Eleven
The Waiters and the Doers

Success comes to those who can dream possibilities and have the courage to believe in those possibilities.

As a sales professional you are part of a very special group of people. You are risk taker. I say that not in the sense of your being a desperate gambler. But rather someone who is willing to take a risk on yourself. In almost all cases you earn your income in whole or part through your ability to generate consistent sales results. In other words you are rewarded solely or in part by the results of your efforts.

Your commissions and bonuses replace the salary or hourly income of your counterparts who seek the security of an income determined solely by job classifications and annual revue. This means you are willing to step forward and put yourself to the test in ways that most others would rather avoid. This willingness to take risks should not be under–appreciated in a world where most people seek above all else safety and security. The almost daily highs and lows of the life of a sales professional is something that has to be lived to be fully appreciated and understood.

The stress and anxiety brought on by customer whims and demands along with the uncertainty of whether or not your product or service will be the chosen one takes its' toll. Putting your knowledge, skills and attitude on the line every-day in order to meet your own or the company's sales objectives isn't easy. In my opinion it puts you in some pretty select company in terms of personal attributes and characteristics. Professional sales practitioners share an unlikely affinity with the explorers, trailblazers and pioneering settlers of the frontier days. Those courageous people who set out for new lands offering new opportunities had to combine unshakable inner resolve with strong personal values in order to persevere, stay-the-course, beat the odds and reach their objectives. They didn't know it and they certainly didn't take the time to label them as such, but it was performance qualities combined with spiritual guidance that were the well-spring from which they drew their courage and determination. While not faced with the same often life threatening challenges as those brave souls you face challenges and obstacles everyday and you too need a well-spring of positive energy from which to draw.

You like all of us need to live the day-to-day reality of the business they're in. You however more so than most, need to keep sight of the dream You have. None of us it's true can touch the stars, but it doesn't mean we should stop reaching for them.

The most successful salespeople I've known share a uniquely determined work ethic that is driven and guided by a strong set of personal values. In a lot of cases it's not the work ethic that separates them from colleagues of equal ability it's the strength of their values. Personal values are a performance quality that when nurtured and adhered to can keep you focused on the right thing to do when others around you might be more inclined to go for whatever is expedient. You must face one immutable fact of your professional life. You need to be pragmatic enough to be able to find a balance between your dreams and the one undeniable reality you face everyday. That is, when your mandate is to bring in sales, you are going to have to come to grips with the idea that it isn't going to happen unless you do what it takes to make it happen. You can't hand your challenges off to a colleague or underling like you could in some other positions. We all know that when it comes to work the world is full of willing people some are willing to do it, while others are willing to let them. I call the people willing to do it the doers and the people willing to let them the waiters. Professional salespeople don't last long unless they are one of the doers.

The waiters of the world are great believers in situations and circumstances. You hear them moaning and groaning about them all the time. They are the people who dwell so much on what they can't do, they never seem to get around to doing what they can. The doers of the world are also great believers in situations and circumstances. When they find themselves faced with ones they don't like they find a way to change them. They are the people too busy doing what they can to think about what they can't.

Anyone who has been a sales professional for any length of time will I'm sure have crossed paths with the waiters and the doers. Every sales team I was ever a part of had some of each type on them. The doers are the ones too busy making things happen to have time to talk about it. The waiters are the ones too busy talking about what they're going to do to ever have time to do it. The challenge for every sales manager is to make sure their salespeople learn by emulating the doers and stay out of ear's reach of the waiters.

Sales professionals who want to rise above the average can't do it with a wait for it way of thinking. You can't be a top producer waiting for opportunity to come knocking you've got to get busy and beat down the doors opportunity hides behind. Waiters try to get by while they wait for things to change for the better. Doers challenge the status quo and aren't afraid to change the way they do things. Waiters are people who wait for good things to happen and worry about bad things that might. Doers don't waste time worrying about what might happen they put their energy into dealing with what is happening. The waiters it seems are content to wait for their break to come. They live by the motto "all good things come to those who wait". Which I think is all very nice but only applicable in practical terms to those who expect to live forever.

The waiters of the world need to be reminded that one of the great tragedies of life is not that it ends too soon, but that we wait so long to begin it. Patience may be a virtue in many careers, but a career in professional sales isn't one of them. In the fast paced and demanding world of professional sales waiting for something good to happen is about as productive as waiting to win the lottery. Just like the waiters who live by their previously mentioned motto, the winners in professional sales have one of their own "the harder I work the luckier I get." They don't wait for their performance to be measured and judged solely by others. They are their own task-masters. They fashion their own goals, objectives and performance standards and critique them honestly and objectively. They refuse to play the blame game. They know the best way to escape their problems is to take the responsibility for finding a way to solve them. When setbacks occur they focus on finding positive solutions not on organizing the witch-hunt to find who or what could be blamed for it. When the going gets tough doers steer clear of the counter productive wallowing in self-pity or self-doubt traps that so many others get themselves mired in. They don't waste physical, mental or emotional energy in self-flagellation on the occasions when they are the authors of their own misfortune. The sales professionals who rise to the top accept one very simple truism when it comes to people and things. They understand and accept the notion that the world they live and work in and the people who inhabit it including themselves are not perfect. They know in spite of the best of intentions mistakes get made by them and by those around them, and they usually get made at the most inopportune times. The difference in the quality of people can always be seen in their reactions to them.

Only people willing to accept the risk of failure can ever hope to succeed. When I first began playing golf I like most people who take up the game spent more than my fair share of time studying the flora and fauna growing in the rough. It was during one of those early treks through the underbrush that I first heard this expression offered as a confidence booster by one of the players in my foursome. He said; remember recovery is ninety percent of the game.

It's an expression that I think applies equally well to the game of golf, the game of life and to the world of professional sales. The message I took from it was that there's little of no benefit in fretting about what got you into the rough, the key was to focus on what you need to do to get out of it. Professional sales practitioners would be wise to heed the advice. It clearly acknowledges that mistakes will be made and there is little to be gained by spending every single minute of every single day trying desperately to figure out how to avoid them. It also got me thinking about the futility of beating myself over the mistakes I would inevitably make in my life if I was committed to going after the promise of what could be. Mistakes are an inevitable bi-product of growth and learning. The only sure way I know of avoiding them is to give in, give up and do nothing. I believe all of us who are committed to making the effort to be all that we can be would rather fail in the pursuit of our ambitions than succeed at being average. Make your mistakes, learn form them and move on. You're not perfect and it's not likely that you ever will be. About the closest most people ever come to being perfect is when they're filling out a job application.

Selling is not an exact science. A large part of being a productive salesperson is listening to, testing and trusting your instincts. It's about using tried and true proven methods for making a sale, but it's also about sensing when to go against the prevailing ways of doing things. Only when you free yourself from the burden of trying to be mistake proof will you be free enough to listen to your instincts.

The doers on every sales team are the ones who face challenges head on using their initiative, resourcefulness and determination. They differ from the waiters who like to think things over plan things out analyze things to the nth degree and then of course wait for the right moment before getting active. Conditions for them never seem just right. Have you noticed that people who delay making decisions or taking actions until all conditions are just right, never seem to be able to find those conditions? Doers don't need to be prodded by people or conditions they just go ahead and take the actions needed to generate positive results. This drive to be active and make things happen is anchored in performance qualities like self-confidence and self-motivation.

They understand how a performance quality like positive visualizing can work to their advantage. They know what a productive influence being able to 'see' the positive results of their actions can be. They have experienced first hand the energy it can create and how instrumental it can be in helping them shake off the down days and get up and get at it. Please note I said; visualize not fantasize. Effective visualizing is based in fact and blends together positive thoughts and constructive actions. One of the things most of us learn as we mature is that identifying what needs to be done and taking the appropriate actions to get it done are two very different things. Visualizing begins with thinking about positive ways of doing things and ends with implementing those thoughts to produce positive results. Dreaming begins and ends with pleasant thoughts about what we could get done if we ever get around to doing it. Waiters fantasize about imaginary scenarios while waiting for them to happen. Doers visualize about the positive outcomes of real life situations while involved in them.

The ability to step back and picture yourself doing what needs to be done to produce a positive result is a very powerful motivator. You have a choice at any given moment to decide what thoughts and images you will use to fill the gap between your ears. If you allow that space to become a directionless vacuum it is likely to fill up with negative thoughts, non-productive images and fears of what might be. If on the other hand you take the initiative to fill that space with positive thoughts and productive images you keep the fears out and let the opportunities in.

Chapter Twelve
Uncover the Opportunities in Change.

Faced with the choice of making changes or proving there's no need to do so, almost everyone it seems immediately gets busy on finding the proof.

Change is the 500lb. gorilla in all our lives. Running and hiding from it isn't very productive and it isn't going to work. Instead, we've got to learn how to work with it and make it work for us. In my experience one of the characteristics prevalent among almost all productive sales professionals is their ability to roll with the punches and work constructively within an environment of continuous change.

Working with change and taking advantage of it means making a commitment to personal growth through continuous learning. As Alvin Toffler said; the illiterate of this century will not be those who can't read and write. It will be those who can't learn, un-learn and re-learn. Working with it means expanding your ability to bring about what you want from life. It has to do with approaching life and living it as a creative pro-active person. The people who are successful in finding ways to make change work for them are always anxious to expand their horizons. They see change as providing the opportunity to do so. When you work with instead of against change you find yourself taking more initiative in seeking it out and you take more personal responsibility for fitting into the changes you find.

Change when it enters your life always brings something

into it, but it also takes something out. It makes demands on you to find the courage to reach out and take hold of something new and different while at the same time it forces you to let go of a lot of the old and familiar. It's unsettling because most of the changes we are asked to make involve things we've worked hard to develop and that have brought us our current level of success. Things like, our knowledge, skills, habits and behaviors.

For that reason many people find change can be unsettling and tough to deal with. They find some changes are tougher than others to make and adjust to. Almost without thinking most of us divide change into two categories and react to it accordingly. When we encounter change that is general in nature and affects everyone we don't ordinarily get our shorts in a knot over it. Not many of us got ourselves into a state of high anxiety and swore vengeance over the introduction of the Internet. We chose in the beginning to either get into it or avoid getting caught up in it. Your personal reaction to it was probably, no big deal either way. We don't see most general changes around us as a threat to us. We just kind of make up our minds to take advantage of them, or continue doing things the way we have in the past. In fact if the changes are general in nature and affect us in a way that makes us happier or healthier we embrace them and accept them without much reaction at all.

It's a very different story when change becomes personal and specific to us. Like a change in the way we are expected to perform our job functions. In that case, most of us during the introduction of the changes we are expected to make tend to be a little reactive, some get a little over-reactive and a few go ballistic. It's when change gets in our face and gets personal that we react by trying to ignore it, fight with it, or hide from it. So it would seem that most of us could be said to be in favor of change, as long as it doesn't actually involve us having to make any. When change does start to rock the recliner in our personal comfort zone we have one of two choices. We can change voluntarily or we can be dragged to the altar of change and sacrificed on it, screaming and kicking all the way. Either way change is going to happen. The speed of change leaves a lot of people feeling a little weary and changed out from time to time. We don't throw our arms open to change because sometimes we just don't feel up to wrestling with the challenges it brings. A lot of people today will tell you they're pretty challenged just getting through the days they're familiar with, without learning how to adapt to new ones. Working with the old and familiar might be the way a lot of people would like it to be, but it isn't the way it's going to be.

There's nothing terribly wrong with wanting to stay the way you are. There's nothing bad about wanting to continue doing the same familiar things in the same familiar ways. There's nothing wrong with just trying to maintain the same customers and market-share you've always had. There's nothing wrong with wanting to be eighteen again either, but in every case, it just isn't going to happen. We are living organisms and we are either in a state of growing or dying there is no staying the same. New technology, economic globalization and demographic shifts will all play a part to ensure that we encounter change at an accelerated rate in the years ahead.

We don't talk anymore about a change or some changes we simply talk about change, as if it has a life of it's own. Today for most of us in our business and personal lives, it's change as far as the eye can see. There is so much change going on around us that we can lose perspective on it. Sometimes we think we invented change. We are the change experts and also the sometimes victims of it. When we're caught up in it we think of it as some new mind-boggling challenge that no one before us had to deal with. On the contrary, people have been adjusting and adapting to change since mankind crawled out of the cave and decided the change from walking on all fours to upright seemed like a good change to make.

Consider this excerpt from an article about the effects of change and attitudes toward it that appeared in a leading magazine back in 1837. Change today seems like the only constant in most people's lives. It becomes more threatening to a lot of people every day. The world around us is becoming more and more complicated. Most of us spend too much of our time and effort and energy just trying to keep up, and the feeling is we just continue getting further behind. Business today is racing ahead at breakneck speed. It heaps changes on us so quickly we sometimes stumble under the weight of them. Everywhere we turn it seems like there is more pressure to get more done in less time.

Some would have you believe that today, in order to deal effectively with the accelerated pace of change we need to develop a new and radical mind-set toward it. We need to find new ways to manage it. But do we really, are things really all that different. The things in your life today that you consider normal, everyday, and mundane, were probably at sometime in someone's life radical and challenging change.

I can promise you this, there is nothing in the life of professional sales practitioners as constant as change. The dynamics of customer relationships are changing all the time. A case in point is the way change has affected our ability to stay in touch with our customers. We've gone from messenger boys, to telegraph to telephone to fax and now Email. Every single customer you deal with is different with his or her wants and needs changing all the time. All of us are faced with the challenge of managing both planned for and unexpected changes thrown at us by our customers. It is vital to your success that you be able to continue to make a positive, and knowledgeable impression on your customers. Your adaptability and willingness to roll with unexpected change and your ability to take full advantage of planned change will have a significant impact on your continued success. You don't need a radical new mind-set to deal with change. As with most things the key to managing it productively is your attitude.

What you need is the willingness to apply the principles of positive attitude to the challenge of change. You need to have the confidence to let your positive attitude and optimistic outlook guide you in finding productive ways to respond to it, and create some of it. I'm a sports fan and I've lived through two distinct eras in sports. When I was young the world of sports was a world filled with continuity and stability. There were fewer teams and fewer players and both teams and players for the most part stayed where they were. Sure some players occasionally got traded, but there was no mass movement like you see today. Today that comfortable world of continuity and stability has changed to reflect the realities of the modern era. It has evolved like the rest of society into a place where change is the norm. Players it seems are on the move all the time, selling their services to the highest bidder. Today, it's the teams that have learned how best to take advantage of change and retool their player rosters on a consistent ongoing basis that are most successful. They get to the top and stay there because they've learned two basic truths. One, fighting with change and doing things the old way, leads to losing. Two, working with change and finding ways to make it work for them, leads to winning.

I think most of you would agree, when we come face to face with specific changes that require a different way of thinking and different ways of doing it is difficult to resist the impulse to fight with them. The impulse is even stronger when the way we've been doing things has been generating satisfactory results. It really comes down to live for the moment or plan for the future. I said earlier in the book; you won't survive long trying to simply protect the status quo. You've got to commit yourself to planned growth through change, because the minute you stop growing, you start dying.

We are all creatures of habit to be sure. Change demands that we leave our well-established warm and fuzzy comfort zones. It forces us to adjust our familiar and comfortably entrenched ways of doing things. Familiarity it would seem doesn't only breed contempt it also breeds comfort. Change almost always opens up new worlds of opportunity to us, but to get there we have to travel uncomfortable and unfamiliar roads. Hundreds of years ago map-makers used to paint dragons on parts of the maps they drew. The dragons were there to indicate where the explored and known areas ended and the unexplored began. In time those areas became known simply and ominously as the lands of the dragons. Anytime we move forward and enter into change we in our own way setting out to conquer unexplored areas, and in so doing we sometimes have to fight some dragons. If people in the past hadn't had the courage and willingness to face up to their dragons, we wouldn't have to go anywhere to visit where we came from, we'd still be there. We'd all be applying for membership in the flat earth society, because they seem like such progressive guys.

Change in our workplace causes us to have to take steps to expand our knowledge and skills, because implementing change usually also means having to make use of new unfamiliar tools, systems and procedures. It causes us to modify and expand our way of thinking and adapt our ways of doing. Change is the kick in the butt, we don't always want, but sometimes need. We need to look at our current status quo, our state of being, as a launching pad not a resting place. We need to have stability when it comes to the personal values and core competencies in our lives but we also need to make sure that same stability does not manifest itself in stagnation of our thoughts and actions.

The ability to manage change is a primary factor in the success of high achieving sales people and has a direct impact on getting to the top and staying there. The inability to manage it contributes to the failure of those who don't. In my experience it is always the top people in any sales organization who are most open to change and who get busy quickly with ways to make it work in their favor. The others waste time resisting it and are slower getting off the mark to make use of it. You don't hear high achieving sales-people espousing the old 'if it ain't broke don't fix it' bromide, they are the ones too busy looking for ways to break it.

Those of us who are getting a little older and grayer like to put a lot of emphasis on the value of experience. You can't replace experience we like to say. Well, it pains me to say this but experience today may not be as valuable a commodity as it once might have been. I once had a football coach who reminded me that practice didn't make perfect, it was perfect practice that made perfect. I think something similar applies to experience. The value of our experience is not in having it, the value lies in how we apply it. If your skills, knowledge and expertise aren't relevant to the demands of the marketplace you work in, the value of your experience is diminished. All else pales and becomes insignificant if you are unable or unwilling to make the changes necessary to continue to position yourself as a useful and valuable resource to your customers.

When you look at change are you looking at it through the eyes of a positive thinking change opportunist or are you your own worst enemy. If you intend to continue to do what you do the way it's always been done, good luck, you don't need to read on. If on the other hand you believe as I do that we can all benefit from being open to new ways of getting things done, read on. Recall if you can some recent circumstances in your life when you have been asked to or had to make a change to the way you'd always done things. Did you jump for joy, or did you start thinking about the change from a negative perspective? Did you start thinking about and making a mental list of the aggravations the change you were asked to make would visit upon you. If you did, relax you're normal. You didn't do the most productive thing, but you did what most of us would do.

The fact is we can only put ourselves in a position to profit from change in our lives when we open our minds to the possibilities they create. Conversely we put ourselves in a position to suffer from the consequences of ignoring change when we close our minds and try to shut ourselves off from the changes around us. All that does is isolate us from opportunity and it keeps us mired in mediocrity. It fools you into thinking you can continue to generate new business using old outdated skills. It's impossible to make new inroads when we resist new ideas and cling to old habits. You end up defending the way it used to be instead of participating in the way it now is. When we close our minds and shut ourselves off it's like closing yourself up in a room without light and locking the door behind you. For a while you feel safe and secure from outside dangers, but sooner or later you realize the biggest danger lies in what you're doing to yourself.

Every sale professional with an open mind and a willingness to embrace and work with instead of against change empowers him or herself to take on new interesting and potentially profitable challenges. Being open to change can help you discover new more creative and productive ways of doing things.

When you develop the habit of reaching out to change instead of trying to push it away, you become more focused on 'why-not' instead of 'why'. Why is a word in search of a problem. We use it too often to put a negative spin on things. It challenges in a negative way. It encourages us to participate in the 'why-whine'. The why-whine is what you hear from people who when challenged by change usually respond by saying; 'why do we have to do it some new way', 'why can't we leave well enough alone', 'why do we keep making so many changes'. It's always 'why this', 'why that', 'why now' and 'why me'. Why-not on the other hand, is a positive call to action, looking for opportunity. 'Why-not try it this way'? 'Why-not give it a chance'? 'Why-not me, I can do it'.

Change doesn't have to be your enemy you can make it your ally by having a never- ending thirst for learning about and trying out new ideas or ways of doing things. One of the most fundamental changes that has been brought about by the shift from a jobs to an initiative based economy is this; success is no longer governed by what you know, it will be driven by what you are willing to learn. You know from your own experiences that your customer's needs and ways of doing business are changing all the time. They are constantly changing the way they use products and services. You might be hoping you can get by on the old, but they are looking for ways to move on to what's new. You better make sure you put yourself in a position to offer them new ideas, and innovative products and services or somebody else will. If you're in the habit of uttering any or all of the following expressions, it probably means that you need to kick your attitude toward change up a notch or two.

- Nobody I know has ever been successful doing that.
- I tried that once, it didn't work.
- I've always done it this way.
- This is the only way it works for me.
- I couldn't do it like that, it's just not me.
- Why in the world would people buy stuff like that?
- I think I'd better think a while longer about this before I make any changes.
- My competitors aren't doing it, why should I?
- It doesn't look to me like all these changes are worth the effort.
- I'm just in a slump, as long as I keep busy things will turn around.
- I guess I should make some changes......but.

There is no greater gift you can give yourself and none that will add more value to your life experience than the willingness to change. Make sure your focus is on what is going to happen not on what already has. We need respect for the past but to live in it is a sure fire recipe for failure. Change creates opportunities, it generates new pleasures, it keeps you growing mentally and emotionally, it keeps your ruts from getting too deep. Get into the habit of asking, why-not when other people talk about why it can't be done.

Chapter Thirteen
Tap Into Your Creativity

Very few people bother to think more than once or twice a year. If you can manage to do it even once or twice a month think of what an advantage you'll have.

A friend once suggested to me, the brain is a wondrous thing. It switches on as soon as we wake up and off as soon as we get to work. Most of us go through the daily fundamentals of everyday living without a whole lot of in depth thinking. What we do over time is fashion a comfortable, effective and efficient way of doing the everyday things in our lives. This enables us to perform them without a lot of conscious thinking. We don't think much about adjusting the water for our shower, how we brush our teeth, or comb our hair, or what we eat for breakfast I mean the choice between corn flakes or raisin bran isn't going to tax the gray matter too much. Once we get a basic handle on the things we do in our daily lives we do about eighty percent of them without thinking. We are creatures of habit. We drive to work the same way. We take our coffee the same way. We mostly follow a pretty set routine for getting through our day.

Once at work a lot of people immediately shut down their brains and go on autopilot for the day. Doing the routine things that are always there to be done, and spending their days reacting in rote fashion to whatever comes their way. We act out of habit. Our habits are formed by repeated behavior over time. The tendency is to repeat the same old behaviors that don't require a lot of thought. Most will even prefer to continue doing things in old familiar and comfortable ways even when new more productive and beneficial ways of doing them are introduced.

A lot of people consider workplace routine a blessing. It frees them up to concentrate on the really important things in their lives. Things like where to take their next vacation or whether the pants they're wearing make their hips look big. Workplace routine is not something that's an option for professional sales practitioners. Your success won't be predicated on being able to fashion routine ways of doing things. Your success will be gained through equal measures of creative thinking and innovative doing. Initiating productive actions to uncover new business and reacting positively and productively to actions driven by customer needs is the constant tug and pull of your day. In fact when things get too routine it should be a red flag warning that business is slowing down, and opportunities aren't being generated.

Professional salespeople usually go through a typical day juggling their time and trying to squeeze more minutes out of the hours. Their day is usually about thinking on the fly and dealing with the unexpected. That's why the most successful are creative thinkers and innovative doers.

To innovate is to bring about productive changes in products services or the way in which we do things. Two things fuel innovation, creative thinking and responding positively to our old friend change. A primary requirement for both is to have a positive and open attitude about the possibilities created by new ways of doing things. Finding innovative new ways of doing things is not the sole jurisdiction of off the wall fly by the seat of your pants business radicals. It needs to be part of the basic tool kit for successful sales people. Discovering new more creative and productive ways of doing things does not usually come about as a result of someone being struck by some out of nowhere flash of inspirational brilliance. They evolve from trial and error and a concentration on thinking about how to get more productivity out of old established ways of doing things. In other words, innovative new ways of doing things is the result of a systematic logical and disciplined attempt to exploit what is and change it into what could be.

Any creative thinking process is grounded in taking a holistic view of situations and circumstances. To make it work, you first have to free yourself from unimaginative 'there's only one-way to do it,' or 'this is the way I've always done it' thinking. You need to broaden your outlook. Instead of a one-dimensional straight-line view of things you need to try looking at them as they might appear through a prism. You need to intentionally distort your view looking at things from every angle and then bring it back into focus.

You also need to make a conscious effort to avoid the grim reapers that are always present whenever creative thinking and innovation dies. The first of the grim reapers is negativity. Your creative juices are not going to flow unimpeded if they are constantly being blocked along the way by negative thoughts and attitudes. You aren't going to do much creative thinking if you're focus is always on 'why it won't', instead of 'why it will'. First cousin to a negative attitude is a cynical outlook. When cynicism is prevalent in our thinking, we are blinded by the cost of everything and we too often miss seeing the value in anything. A cynical outlook usually starts to develop through association with pessimistic people. It starts to impact on our thoughts and actions when Instead of trusting ourselves our abilities and our instincts we make the mistake of listening to and putting too much stock into the opinions of people around us. You must have noticed that pessimists are always standing by at the ready with negative opinions on anything and everybody. Their opinions are offered unsolicited and at no charge. You need to stop now and then and remember the value of their opinions always equals the price you're asked to pay.

Another sure-fire creativity killer is fear of failure. When fear of failure is allowed to dominate your decision making process it leads you away from creative thinking and innovative actions and back toward protection of the status quo. It can cause you to be afraid to convert your creative thoughts into innovative actions and new ways of doing things. Instead of having the courage to reach out for what could be, you end up settling for just making do with the way it is. We justify having a fear of failure by convincing ourselves that to try and to fail is somehow equal to being stupid or incompetent. In most cases we aren't afraid of failing as much as we're afraid of being branded a failure. Allow me if you will a personal insight here. People who fail in the pursuit of innovation and improvement are never failures. The only failures are people who never challenge themselves because they're too afraid to fail. I've stared into the face of failure and I can tell you from personal experience, it is not a pretty sight. But it's not something you should be afraid of either. You can't take advantage of the opportunities around you, or do much creative thinking or take many innovative actions if your fear of failure causes you to seek the safety of accepting things the way they are. How you recover from your mistakes is so much more important than spending every single waking minute of every single day trying desperately to figure out how to avoid them. What you should be afraid of is having your drive and determination to succeed undermined by unfounded and imagined fears of failing. One sure fire way to avoid falling into that trap is to do a lot less thinking about what might happen if you try new things and get busy trying them.

The last of the creativity killers is coloring inside the lines all of the time. We all have 'our' way of getting things done. As a result, it's easy to fall into habits that hamper our success. One way to do it is by creating self–restricting, creativity and innovation killing personal comfort zones. Sometimes we do get the urge to try innovative and hopefully more productive ways of doing things. Then we get a grip on ourselves and stop because we feel safer and more comfortable doing them the old way. So what if the old comfortable way of doing is only generating average results. You can always adjust and learn to live and get by on just being average. If that's all you want.

In my early years as a golfing duffer I was able because of having some athletic ability to play at an average level of proficiency. After a few years I became comfortable and content to play at that level by playing the way I had always played. There came a time however, when I wanted to improve my game. To make those improvements I was going to have to change things. I was going to have to drag myself out of my comfort zone cocoon and do things differently. I put off making the necessary changes to my game. I struggled with the idea of having to color outside the lines. I was going to have to make adjustments to my grip. I was going to have to adjust my swing. I was going to have to think differently and take different actions. If I was going to get my score down I was going to have to endure the pain of going outside my personal parameters. I had to accept the reality of short-term pain for the hoped for long-term gain. To my surprise and delight the pain of having to make the adjustments and the jolt to my ego of having to suffer the corresponding inflation of scores was short lived. The long-term gain of lowered scores and more enjoyment from the game continues to this day. If I had not had the want to improve and the determination to learn how I would have continued to play within my self imposed limitations and never have enjoyed the satisfaction of improved performance. Life can be a lot like that. Most of us figure out somewhere along life's learning curve that in order to generate different and improved results, we first have to learn and apply different ways of doing.

Once in a while it's time well spent to apply some creative thinking to what you do and how you do it. You always benefit when you take steps to get yourself out of any self-imposed rut. The best way to do it is to look at ways to bend, fold, reshape, and make changes to the way you've always thought about and done things.

One key reason why it's so important for salespeople to think creatively and innovate systematically is this; every product or service you sell has a distinct life cycle consisting of five stages; introduction, growth, maturity, decline and expiration. You're on the front lines everyday. You're the eyes and ears of your company. You've got to keep your eyes and ears open to learn when your customers are telling you that you've reached the limits of a particular product or service life cycle. There may come a point in time when the market becomes saturated and the upside potential for new customers declines. There may even come a time when the organization you represent should pursue a new product or service line rather than spending all their time and resources on improving what you have. If what you have is not what people want, improving it isn't going to increase the demand for it. Just to make things a little more challenging the speed of today's changes and advances and the volume of information being disseminated means the time between the stages in product and service life cycles is getting shorter.

Don't resist making the effort to innovate and think creatively because you believe the product or service you sell is unique and only you can provide it. In today's marketplace, that's like standing back and congratulating yourself on building a 386 computer. I repeat; no one person and no one organization can prosper long in today's fast changing marketplace when your mandate is to protect what you have without also going after what you don't.

Sticking our collective heads in the sand or whistling through the graveyard hoping things won't change or nobody's chasing us is a sure fire recipe for disaster. Creative thinkers and innovative action takers not only expect to encounter unexpected change they make an effort to cause their fair share of it. A personal or organizational strategy based solely on capturing and maintaining a piece of the existing pie instead of looking for ways to get a piece of emerging new pies is just not an option. Over time you will find that instead of attacking your competitors and capturing new market share you will be fighting an organized retreat as your customer base and market share decline to the point where you and your business become irrelevant.

Why is it that some salespeople are able to fashion a good couple of years of sales and then fade into mediocrity or obscurity. One reason could be, they put too much focus on the present, with little or no thought to the future. They put all their energies into what is and little or none into what is going to be. On the other hand people who are consistently at the top of their game have the drive and determination to maximize what is, but they also balance those qualities with the creative zeal to consistently welcome and seek out change and innovation in their personal package of skills and their product or service mix.

About one hundred years ago when I was taking what was then called the commercial program in high school, a course called business machines was part of the curriculum. Each student enrolled in the course was required to learn the basic operating procedures of the business machines that were in common use in offices of the 1960's. These cutting edge business tools consisted of things like electric typewriters and electronic calculators. The manufacturers of these business machines fully expected them to be the backbone of office operations for years to come. One of the things that became very obvious to many of us in the course was that the machines were incredibly limited in what they could do, and they were awkward to use, noisy and slow.

At that time there were many competitors making and selling office business machines. One company in particular specialized in one high quality line of electronic calculators. Their product line was well respected and they enjoyed significant market share. For the purposes of this story we will call the company Premier Business Machines.

Graduates from the high school commercial course going directly into the work force could expect to find employment working in accounting, billing, and administration departments surrounded by a sea of Premier Business Machines. By the late 60's all was well in the land of Premier Business Machines. Market share was strong and demand for their products was constant. Their salespeople really became more like order takers. They looked after the needs of their existing customers to the exclusion of going after new customers. New customers came to them, they didn't need to go out looking. No one at that time and most certainly not the people in the research and development department of P.B.M. ever suspected that times they were a'changin. No one ever imagined in the safe and comfortable world of P.B.M. that some new fangled machine called a computer would limit the life cycle of their product line and make it redundant and obsolete in the not too distant future.

When the new computer technology was in its infancy some creative and innovative companies recognized its potential to create a whole new 'way of doing business' and began to work toward putting themselves in a position to profit from it. Premier Business Machines wasn't one of them. Why should they? They were a world-wide giant in the field of electronic calculators. Celebrated for their quality and continuous improvements to their traditional product line. They weren't keeping an eye on any new fangled pie in the sky technology. Their focus was on beating the current competition and protecting their current market share. They were hell bent on producing and selling the best line of electronic calculators known to man. The research and development boys took to their bunkers, hunkered down and redoubled their efforts to turn out the definitive electronic calculator. In all likelihood they did! But no one will ever know, because just about the time they were ready to unleash their newest calculator the market began to change. The calculator was out. The computer was in. P.B.M. was nowhere. P.B.M. management had failed to come to grips with the idea that creative thinking and innovative actions could invent the office of the future and bring it into the present. The past now belonged to P.B.M. The lesson here is; they had been too busy fighting the other alligators in the swamp to notice the swamp was drying up. We all need a process for helping us think creatively and innovate consistently if we are going to compete successfully.

Machiavelli wrote; 'I have often reflected that the causes of the successes or failures of men depend upon their manner of suiting their conduct to the times'. Nothing could be truer in this era of rapid change and ongoing marketplace innovation. Creative thinking combined with a consistent search for innovative actions leads to the exploitation of opportunity. Together they can solidify our determination and fuel our imagination. By being creative and innovative we can reach new levels of personal performance.

Any process for helping us think more creatively must begin by making sure we don't focus exclusively on the minutia of everyday problems and miss bigger picture opportunities. Problem solving is to treading water what creative thinking is to swimming for shore. It is a given that if you fall out of the boat you have to keep afloat or drown. Treading water is a necessary but short-term solution. It addresses the immediate problem at hand, but unless you also have a plan for making headway toward land chances are you aren't going to survive. Obviously we all need to respond to and solve everyday problems. However, becoming mired in the moment too often results in limiting your focus, ideas and thoughts on immediate survival instead of long term prosperity. If you're into the quick fix, you will always be focused exclusively on each problem as and when they are encountered. If you see yourself only as a hammer then you will tend to look at every problem only as a nail. If all your energies are focused on solving problems then you are bound to overlook the opportunities that often lie buried within them. We all overlook potential sources of opportunity everyday in our ongoing and it seems never ending, battle to manage situations and solve problems.

After 30 years of selling something to somebody I still get excited about making a successful sale. Maybe it's the competitive nature of the beast or the stroking of ego, or the revenue generated but every sale makes me want to make more. One of the best times for me to do some creative thinking is right after making a sale. I always ask myself how can I leverage the just completed sale into more like it. Then I go though the following exercise to help me think creatively. The objective of the exercise is to identify possible sources of new or additional business. The source of where the creative thought originates or the type of innovative actions required to put it into play don't matter. It's not important whether an idea or opportunity comes from an unexpected source, a strength or weakness or whether it is original, adapted or borrowed. You don't get any points for neatness in this process. The idea of the exercise is to identify opportunities no matter the source.

- What if anything did my three most recent sales have in common?
- What can I do to leverage those sales with similar customers?
- What prospects and customers in my sales territory are generating the most current business?
- What do I think is the primary reason for the response?
- Which new market sectors have I experienced the most success with lately?
- What can I do to contact more customers in those market sectors?
- What if any totally unexpected companies or groups have purchased my services in the last quarter?
- How did they find out about me?
- What new market sectors company wide are generating the most sales or interest in my product or service at this time?
- What should I be doing to capitalize on this interest?
- What is the primary reason I have been able to penetrate new market sectors?

Chapter Fourteen
Find the Excitement in Doing

Sometimes I lie awake at night wondering 'why me'.
Then I hear a voice answer, 'nothing personal
your name just happened to come up'.

How you manage your performance qualities will have an enormous and continuous impact on your success personally and professionally. The challenge most of us face is not in identifying and labeling the qualities we need to have, that's easy. The real challenge lies in finding our way of continuously refining them and applying them in productive and manageable ways. Knowing what to do, and knowing how to do it productively and consistently are two very different things. On the golf course I know how to hold my putter, how to line up my putt and how to stroke the ball. I can do all of that with reasonable proficiency, but I still register too many three-putt greens because I cannot do it with the consistency of a really good player. The result is in most cases a less than productive and satisfying round of golf.

One performance quality, that comes to mind right away and has a significant impact on how we think, how we act and what we ultimately achieve is the degree of passion we have for what we do and the level of passion we have for it while doing it. In every sales driven environment your level of passion for what you do will influence your day to day work habits and impact on your long term level of success. Simply put, you need to be excited about who you are, what you do, and how you do it. I don't mean you have to approach your prospects and customers with the manic exuberance of a Robin Williams let loose in front of an audience. But you do need to find your way of having and showing genuine excitement about yourself and your product or service. Enthusiasm is contagious Spent your time with others who have it. Genuine excitement about your product or service goes a long way to increasing your prospect or customers confidence in who you are and what you represent. The flip side and one we all need to make a conscious effort to avoid is spending too much time in the company of people who are largely lethargic and have a kind of sluggish look and aura about them. If you spend enough time with them you too begin to feel your energy being sapped. An example that comes to mind, and one I think we can all relate to is finding yourself in the company of someone who begins to yawn. The next thing you know you're sitting slack jawed and sucking in air right along with them. The thing to keep in mind is, our actions have an effect on the energy level of those around us just as their actions influence us.

If you believe as I do that the primary objective of any sales process is to match your product or service to the need of the customer and then present them with a compelling reason to take action, take it now and take it with you, then you will also agree with me when I say that one of the strongest influences on your prospect or customer's buying decision will be your passion for what you do and what you sell. Whenever I give a speech part of what I am doing is selling ideas and thoughts to the audience. I consider it a great compliment when people say not only did they learn from what I was saying, but they got caught up in the way it was being said. I often have people come up to me after a speech and say, "boy are you ever passionate about what you're saying", or "you look like you're really enjoying what you do". Yes, I do have fun and I do enjoy what I do, because I have a passion for what I do while I'm doing it and I'm passionate about the message I am delivering.

Enthusiasm for the moment, excitement for the situation

and a passion for what they do, are attributes shared by almost all successful sales professionals. It's important to note here that having a passion for what you do and being passionate about doing it are not one in the same. We are told over and over by the gurus of personal empowerment and self-management that in order to truly tap into our talents and make the most of our abilities and feel really fulfilled as individuals we have to find something to work at that will create a passion within us. I believe the opposite.

I to believe that in an ideal world we would all be working at something that fires us up, creates a passion within us and that we could get excited about all day every day. Now having said that, I'm not sure about the world you live in but the one I spend my time in has a ways to go before we can all be working at the perfect job. So instead of being frustrated about not being one of he lucky ones who are doing something that creates a passion within us, what we all have to do is find ways to either be passionate about whatever it is that we do, or the results we achieve while doing it. In other words a lot of us who may not have the luxury of having a choice in terms of what we do, or who may not be doing what we would really enjoy or want to do, can make ourselves happier and more productive by finding ways to enjoy what we do, or the results of what we accomplish. You don't have to love it, just find a way to have some fun with it and get some enjoyment from it and some passion for it just might slip in along the way.

Early in my selling career I worked as a salesperson for a company that manufactured envelopes. Now I can tell you from first hand experience it's pretty tough to get passionate about selling envelopes. I called on large user accounts like direct mail houses, government departments, banks and department stores. I wasn't passionate about the commodity I was selling but I was very passionate about the commissions I was earning, and the lifestyle those commissions made possible. Don't let anyone tell you that a good salesperson always looks past the commissions and thrives only on doing a good job for their customers or clients. Being driven by the passion of earning a good income while satisfying the needs of your customers is as far as I'm concerned a very professional and ethical way of doing business. Besides, anyone with a misplaced sense of passion for the sale alone, over and above what's good for their customers isn't going to last long, make quality sales or earn high commissions anyway.

Sometimes passion is mislabeled and misunderstood. In my experience the bigger the organization the more entrenched the mind-set. The management of too many large companies that become complacent and begin to believe in their own infallibility end up developing a culture that succeeds more often in spite of and not because of how they think and what they do. Instead of being the innovators they become the duplicators. Over time they fall into the destructive trap of fixating on protecting the status quo, and safely following while others are boldly leading. In those organizations straight jacket thinking resonates from the top down. In these corporate dead zones stoicism is celebrated as a workplace virtue. Just do it, don't think about it, is the order of the day. Lead, follow or get out of the way is replaced by; follow the leader or make way for someone who will. Individual passion, emotion and excitement are characterized as loose cannon weaknesses and the concept of teamwork exists not to encourage individual innovative input but only to meet the pre-set objectives of management. Oh sure you are expected to get excited about the latest corporate initiative or passionate about the most recent edict from on high, but step up and show any genuine emotion or originality in the way you think and do and you are soon looked at as someone to be wary of.

In a work world where originality is too often looked on as rocking the boat and fitting in is admired more than standing out the passionate are in true Pavlovian style soon conditioned to respond with excitement and interest only to corporate stimulus, and rewarded accordingly. In our culture, stoicism is looked at as a virtue, right there along side loyalty. The long suffering admired for their perseverance and tenacity in sticking it out. Too many times, in too many companies the best and the brightest are driven out by the confines of fitting in. They leave in search of less bureaucratically-bound places to work. Place where they can recapture their passion and be stimulated by their workplace. While at the same time, those who's sole ability is to stick it out and go with the flow are rewarded. That's why too many old economy companies find themselves with too many bureaucratic thinkers and too few passionate doers. Never mistake big for bright.

Waking up in the morning and looking forward to what you do and the rewards of doing it and feeling passionately excited and emotionally and spiritually positive about what you have a chance to accomplish sure beats the heck out of being what I call a flat-liner. Flat-liners are people who go through life keeping their emotions in check, never getting too up or too down and taking what life gives, instead of striving for what life offers.

There are lots of dividends to be cashed when you make a commitment and put in the effort to find your personal, professional and spiritual passion. Your taste for life gets sweeter. The downs you encounter are easier to adjust to, deal with and overcome. You begin to see them in a different light and you are better able to put them into the proper perspective. They become speed bumps on your road to success, not the insurmountable barriers they might have once appeared to be. Sure, they will from time to time slow you down and cause you to re-evaluate your priorities and ways of thinking and doing, but they are no longer permanent roadblocks with the power to stop you.

When you discover and begin to use your new-found passion to fuel your professional and personal life you will find yourself living in, making the most of and enjoying the present, with less time spent anxiously worrying about the future, or longing for the past. One of the things I have to take time to remind myself of is, life is not a practice run. We can all to easily fall into the trap of being too busy to appreciate what John Lennon meant when he said; "life is what happens, while we're busy making other plans".

Passion, excitement, positive emotion and spirituality, are tributaries coming together to increase your flow of constructive energy. Every sales practitioner starts out with potential. In order to first tap into it and then maximize it, you need to be able to find a way to work at higher levels of energy for longer periods of time than people in less stressful and demanding jobs. Customers may enjoy the luxury of being tired and cranky, but not the salesperson. I didn't make the rules it's just the way it is. Customers want to see and sense from salespeople physical, mental and emotional energy during the selling process. It might not make any sense but very often the customer will subconsciously associate the salesperson's' enthusiasm and energy with the quality and performance of the product.

Someone once said that the world is a stage and most of us are desperately under rehearsed. When a salesperson begins his or her presentation he or she is required to put on a positive energetic audience pleasing performance. The degree of energy you put into your presentation will in a lot of cases be one of the contributing factors to the success or failure of it. The enthusiasm you bring to your sales presentation is directly influenced by the passion you have for what you are doing at the time of doing it.

Finding your passion for what you do will always help you produce and maintain the high levels of energy required to respond productively to the physical, mental and emotional demands of professional sales. A high level of physical energy is demanded by the hours most salespeople put in. Mental energy is required to juggle the countless demands on your time that come into play on a daily basis. A higher than average emotional energy level is needed to help respond to and adjust to the various whims and demands of a typically diverse customer base. The more passion, the more energy the more positive will be your presentation. Let's not forget that in sales you can't win them all. When you lose it's the energy generated in part by your passion that lets you get over the loss more quickly and refocus your efforts on creating your next opportunity to win.

When the going gets tough the tough get going. That's all well and good but tough has nothing to do with it. It's your strength of personal commitment and your determination to stay at it that makes the difference. Having a passion for what you do and being excited about the way you do it, produces an outlook that is enthusiastic, realistic, optimistic and positive. It helps you map out constructive courses of action that are focused, practical and workable. It doesn't mean looking at life through rose-colored glasses or blithely smiling in the face of adversity. On the contrary it means going head on with the challenges you face. It helps you mix and match your talent, skills, knowledge and attitude to craft workable solutions to both the ordinary everyday challenges we all face along with the extraordinary problems we sometimes encounter.

Chapter Fifteen
Strengthen Your Self-Confidence

*To me the epitome of lack of confidence is a
church steeple with a lightning rod attached.*

Self-confidence is the antidote to self-doubt. Why is that important to sales professionals? It's important because in the world of professional sales, self-doubt is a destroyer, self-confidence a builder. You can only ever be as positive as you make up your mind to be. The message is clear. We have direct control over how we think, what we think about, and the corresponding actions generated by our thoughts. Most of us don't go through life waiting for random things to occur and then reacting to them. Sure, sometimes random occurrences happen and occasionally we act on random impulses but for the most part things we involve ourselves in are things we've given some thought to. In other words, most of the time we look before we leap.

We think about the pros and cons of our actions before taking them and we almost always weigh the hoped for positive results against the hoping to be avoided negative consequences. How does this impact on a typical sales process? Part of the selling process is helping your customers identify a need that can be addressed by using your product or service. All successful salespeople learn to articulate the unique features of their product or service and turn them into customer benefits. They are able to help their customers see the positive results gained by using their product or service and how they can avoid the negative consequences of not using them. The only way to make that happen consistently is to have confidence in yourself and your product or service. You have to be convinced of and able to communicate a genuine belief that your product or service can and will benefit your customers and that you stand behind the performance of them.

If you're not sold, you'll never be successful selling it to your customers. Any consistently successful selling process rests on the ability of the salesperson to first generate positive thoughts in their own mind, about the benefits of doing business with them. Only when their confidence in themselves is rock solid will they be able to transfer their confidence in the integrity of their product or service to their customers.

I would not describe the high achieving sales professionals I know as shrinking violets hesitant to recognize or enjoy their success. Successful salespeople and rightly so, are always the first to give themselves a well-earned pat on the back. It's not an arrogant I'm better than you, in your face type of self-celebration. It's more like a 'hey', I knew I could do it, and I did, style of self–congratulation which contributes to their self-esteem and increases their self–confidence. One particular characteristic I've observed in almost all high achieving salespeople is their understanding of the power of positive reinforcement and its resulting impact on their self-confidence. Because they play everyday on the field of win and lose, they learn to appreciate the value in focusing on and appreciating the thrill of victory and getting over as quickly as possible the disappointment of defeat. Focusing on the former increases confidence, dwelling on the latter develops self-doubt.

I think most professional sales practitioners will agree with me when I say they work in a black and white world with little or no room for gray areas. You make the sale or you don't. A sale made is a win. A sale missed is a loss. They learn to accept and appreciate the accolades they receive from their company or customers for a job well done. There is nothing self-centered or vain in having your ego stroked by people who appreciate your talent and effort You are out there on the limb everyday so my advice is to learn to enjoy the moment because those of us who have been there can attest to the validity of the words of the song made famous by Frank Sinatra; "you can be flyin high in April and shot down in May, but that's life". It's a world where the pendulum swings dramatically between recognition and rejection. Never look a gift horse in the mouth. Positive reinforcement from people around you can be very effective and motivating. Especially when it's grounded in sincerity and offered from people with empathy for what you are trying to accomplish. It can have even more dramatic impact and make a longer lasting impression on you when it's self-generated.

We've all been recipients of compliments from others that are well meant but obviously lacking in sincerity. They're still positive reinforcement but the impact on us is negligible. Even sincere compliments and awards, while fun to receive hold the potential of being harmful in the long term if not viewed in the proper context. They do it's true contribute to increased self-esteem and make a significant contribution to positive reinforcement of the efforts we make but measuring our success only in terms of what others reward us with can lead to too much reliance on outside validation of your worth. In the long term it can be risky and can even be self-defeating to allow recognition from others and outside positive reinforcement alone to have total control over what we think of ourselves. A constant craving for outside recognition and positive reinforcement can manifest itself by lessening our self-reliance and increasing our reliance on outside influences, altering the way we think and the actions we take. It's no longer about what we believe in, it becomes all about what we think others want us to believe. It's no longer about taking actions based on our experiences and the instincts we trust instead it becomes all about only taking actions based on what others deem acceptable.

On those occasions when we find ourselves falling into the trap of basing our self-worth exclusively on the opinion of others it's good to step back and remind ourselves that you can't please everyone, so you've got to please yourself. Personally in my experience I've found that not only can't you please all of the people all of the time, but it's a challenge just to please some of the people some of the time. Understand that outside positive reinforcement is based at best on what people see of you in a given situation under a particular set of circumstances. Good or bad what they are judging you on may or may not be the same as what they would see under differing circumstances. You are the only one capable of seeing or understanding the real person behind the way you think or the actions you take. The positive reinforcement you give yourself through a well earned pat on your own back may not be as widely acclaimed as winning the salesperson of the month contest but it should have more meaning.

The link between having a positive outlook and inner self-confidence is profound and meaningful. Developing and putting into practice a strong and meaningful positive outlook is the first small step in gaining the confidence you need to face and overcome the challenges present in any sales career. It takes a confident professional to master the intricacies of any consistently productive selling process.

Self-confidence is the great freedom provider. When you develop a more confident you, you give yourself the gift of flexibility in thinking and doing. In turn this will expand your options, increase your opportunities and create more chances to succeed. The higher your confidence level the less likely you are to lock yourself into only one way of thinking or one way of doing. When what you see is filtered through a strong positive outlook and secure self-confidence you are less likely to be afraid to experiment or change your personal recipe for success and you aren't hesitant to take new unexplored paths on life's journey.

By combining the two elements positive outlook and self-confidence we forge the courage to respond more readily to unanticipated events in our lives. We are more willing and able to make whatever changes in our thinking and ways of doing that are needed to respond productively to any new challenges we might face. They give us the courage we need to walk the road less traveled or break new ground. When confronted with demanding situations you find yourself better able to respond with positive thoughts and constructive actions. Other less confident people faced with the same challenges are tempted to throw in the towel, and give up on themselves.

Self-confidence gives you the freedom and the will to adjust your ambitions upward. People with little self-confidence tend to limit their boundaries. They convince themselves there is nothing wrong in making things easy for themselves and settling for the average results they achieve. People who won't make the effort to develop their confidence inevitably end up undervaluing themselves and operate on a safety first basis of, if I don't try, I can't fail, instead of, if I do try, I might succeed.

A young friend of mine spent three long years trying to develop a line of software for one particular sector of the Internet. Like a lot of small business entrepreneurs he had to find a way to divide his time between trying to generate revenue to meet the payroll, do the administrative work, work hands on with the programmers and do whatever it took to keep his fledgling young business alive. In other words like most aspiring entrepreneurs he wasn't just working twenty-four, seven, he was trying to find a way to work twenty-six, eight. He invested three years of work going down one path and focusing on one specific product line, only to realize that because of the pace of change, the market for those products was quickly drying up.

It would have been easy to give up and become frustrated and bitter by the speed of change in his target sector that was suddenly making his product obsolete. Instead he called on his positive outlook and self-confidence to sustain him and give him the courage to face the new challenges he faced. He had to adjust his thinking and ways of doing and to it quickly. The only way to keep his business afloat was to turn his attention and efforts to developing a completely new line of products for a different business sector. He and his five other colleagues turned their attention to developing products for the E-commerce sector of the Internet. They spent the next four years developing product and building a customer base. They slowly and at times painfully grew into a small but respected player in their market sector. By the time we celebrated his thirtieth birthday last year, his company had grown to employ thirty-five people. Six months after the birthday celebration we celebrated again when his company was sold to a much larger multi-national company for a sum of money that would make a Saudi Prince envious. Some people to this day say he was lucky, maybe luck played a part, we all need a little luck now and then, but I've always believed he is the perfect example of the harder you work the luckier you get. My friend is a great example of how confidence manifests itself in a willingness to adjust to, take advantage of and create change. Confidence builds on itself because through the process of increasing your self-confidence you learn more about the limitlessness of your own abilities.

The word confidence traced back to its' roots means with faith. Confidence gives you the faith to believe in yourself and your ability to reach your goals. Faith in your abilities makes it easier to believe in yourself. My favorite story about confidence and faith has to do with a mountain climber who one day during a climb falls off a steep ledge and begins to plummet to certain death on the rocks over 3,000 feet below. As he is falling he reaches out desperately and miraculously his right hand grabs hold of the only tree branch sticking out of the rocky face of the cliff. As he is hanging there clinging desperately to the branch he begins yelling for help. After a few minutes a booming voice says; "I am here, do you have faith." The climber is momentarily stunned but yells out, "yes I have faith, boy do I ever have faith, I am faith personified." The voice then says; "let go and I will help you". The climber thinks about that for a minute, then asks; "is there anyone else up there I could maybe have a word with?"

When your self-confidence is strong, you work through your days with a feeling of personal empowerment and profound faith in your talents and abilities. You begin to see your world in terms of a selection of options each one well within your grasp. You sense your comfort level growing in terms of who you are and what you do. Your determination to succeed increases and you are more likely to be able to bring your work and home life into harmony. Instead of pushing yourself to succeed you begin to feel like you are being pulled toward success. You begin to feel like you've found the rhythm for working with your job instead of at it. You feel more in control of what you can control and more tolerant and accepting of what you can't. You find yourself less likely to let the present slip by unnoticed and unappreciated. You begin to understand how to build your success from the inside out and that once you master that success in your chosen endeavors will naturally follow. When your self-confidence is strong, you feel physically and emotionally braver and realize there is less in your life to be afraid of. You are still driven to accomplish all that you can, but at the same time you are more accepting of the person you are.

Have you ever just looked at someone and thought to yourself, she looks really confident, or he looks like he's full of confidence. Confident people radiate their confidence through their appearance and body language. They know their strengths and their capabilities, and they focus their thoughts on how to use them to their advantage. In other words they are selective in what they think about. Confident people work on keeping themselves psychologically and mentally prepared to deal positively with the everyday challenges of living a productive life.

Self-confident people can't prevent random negative thoughts from occurring or control unexpected problems from cropping up any more than anyone else. But what they do better than most is manage them. Have you ever been in the company of people who say things like; "gee I hope things work out and I get the sale, or with some luck I'm hoping I might get the contract." I never discount the importance of luck we all need some and it seems like we all get our fair share both good and bad. When it comes to luck the difference as I see it is this; when your confidence level is high it's still nice to get lucky, but you don't wait for it and you don't plan on it. You don't wait for things to happen, you have a practical plan of action designed to put yourself into the type of situations and circumstances that are bound to result in productive things happening. When positive thinking, self-confident people devise a selling strategy they begin with a plan then they put their plan to work by committing to a series of actions that are designed to bring about positive results. In other words they have the determination to do what it takes to make their plan work.

They don't waste time hoping things will happen they invest their time making things happen. Self-confident people spend less time hoping to succeed and more time expecting too. When you're brimming with confidence you are able to present a calm, self assured, knowledgeable and positive image to others. They in turn they are much more likely to respond to your thoughts, ideas and suggestions in positive ways. When your self-confidence is firing on all cylinders you are more selective about the thoughts you let in and the comments you let out. A high confidence level gives us the will to compete and win because with it we are encouraged to see ourselves as winners. When we operate with a high level of confidence we allow ourselves to raise our level of expectation.

How do you top up your confidence level, when it's down a quart or two? You do it by re-focusing on your values and your beliefs. Sometimes you need to read a book or an article about how people just like you have overcome obstacles in their lives and gone on to enjoy success. Call on like-minded positive people around you, to help you get back on track. Most important of all, sit down and think about your strengths and abilities and remind yourself of your accomplishments both big and small at both work and play.

Take a personal achievement inventory once in a while. We've all accomplished much more than we give ourselves credit for. Start your personal achievement inventory by making a list of your lifetime achievements. Start as far back as winning that three-legged race at the school fair. Look back at all the personal and professional wins you've had. It's never too late to give yourself credit for jobs well done. Think about events that turned out well, even though they may have filled you with anxiety going in. Also, accept the fact that if you're going to make things happen, you're also going to question your actions from time to time. Review your actions and make the necessary adjustments needed but don't wallow in mistakes made.

Start believing in yourself again. Make up your mind to take ownership and responsibility for your thoughts, behaviors and actions and the results they generate. Be accepting of people who are empathetic and want to help you help yourself, but be wary of people who are sympathetic and want to help you wallow in self-pity. Don't be influenced by people or friends who are willing to settle for average. People who have succeeded nicely in convincing themselves that average in life is what they are willing to settle for. People who accept that based on the effort they're willing to put in, average is the return they're prepared to take out. The complexity of competing in the world of professional sales makes it almost impossible to strive only for average results and survive for long. A professional sales practitioner has to have the courage and confidence to challenge him or herself to raise the bar after reaching each new level of success. I know lots of examples of sales professionals who worked hard to get their career established and succeeded in reaching their initial goals and objectives, but then they worked equally hard at convincing themselves they weren't talented enough or ready or willing to put in the effort to take their sales to the next level. Instead they focused their efforts on maintaining the status quo. Their objective would be to generate the same sales or perhaps a small increase from the same customers each year. "Oh, I'll be happy to just do what I did last year, or maybe increase it a little" was what they would tell me when we talked. Unfortunately in any sales driven business there is no such thing as maintaining the status quo or staying the same. If you aren't increasing your sales and market share you can be sure you're competitors are.

In almost every case I know of when a sales professional goes into a maintenance mode they find that within 12 months their sales begin to decline. There is no staying the same, you go forward or you fall back. Anyone who has ever made ar living as a salesperson will attest to the idea that to succeed long term you need to make the effort to consistently increase sales within your established customer base and continue to broaden your customer base where and whenever possible. Some wait to long to understand that most basic fact of sales life.

Others wait too long to understand that to stand still is to invite decline, and when the downward sales spiral begins how difficult it is to stop it. Some try to deny the obvious effects of the decline in their sales and corresponding income. They think they can just ride out what they convince themselves is only a temporary dip in sales. They wait for the turnaround to happen, but they don't do what it takes to make it happen. Some manage the situation by adjusting their goals, objectives and life style downward to one that reflects their new reality. Some try after a couple of years to re-ignite, their drive and determination, but most find they've lost a lot of their early confidence and this results in their inability to regain the levels of success they had once enjoyed.

Whether your income is generated by solely by commission or any combination of salary, bonus and commission the bottom line on how much you make is up to you. There are no limits, just as there are no guarantees. You have to take up the challenge, nobody else is going to earn your income for you. As I mentioned earlier in the book you may be part of a team but in almost every case you are paid for your individual accomplishments within the framework of that team. You're the one who has to take the responsibility to keep striving for and attaining new levels of success. Sometimes we get knocked down when we reach up. Sometimes our confidence gets shaken for the moment. It's easy to be confident when we lock ourselves into using old skills, knowledge and attitudes in the same old ways to achieve the same old results. But in order for our confidence to grow and in order for us to trust it we have to keep testing it.

I often suggest to salespeople that they think of the sales opportunities they generate during a business year like ballplayers do with the games they play during a typical baseball season. Baseball players will tell you that over a 162 game schedule most teams are almost certain to win about 70 games and they are also going to for any combination of reasons lose about 70 games. Its what they do in the other 22 that makes the difference between a great year and an average one. The winning teams don't let the losses affect their confidence, they know they are playing a game where you are going to win some and lose some. The goal of the players on every team is to continue to work hard to put themselves in a position to win the games that make the difference. You're not going to win every sales opportunity by closing every sale, but you're not going to lose every one either. The difference between a winning and losing year for you will hinge on your ability to maintain your confidence, bounce back from the losses and continue to generate selling opportunities.

Why is it that our failures haunt us and our successes are too quickly forgotten? I play golf with people who shoot a great round and take all my money and then instead of talking about all the great shots they made spend all their time at the nineteenth hole fixated on whining about the two putts they missed.

Like a lot of things with moving parts you need a maintenance program designed to keep your self-confidence in optimal working order. Do you ever feel in spite of your best efforts to put a positive step forward, that you sometimes become a lightning rod for stress and negativity? I know I do. There are going to be times when in spite of our very best efforts it's going to be our turn in the barrel. That's why it's beneficial and productive to consistently remind ourselves of our accomplishments. We need to remind ourselves not only of the positive outcomes we've generated, but also the steps we took to accomplish them. Celebrate, celebrate dance to the music. We need to invest more time celebrating the good in our lives and less time brooding about the bad. I find it interesting that in the hustle and bustle world we live in with so little time and so much to do, how often when we do get a precious few moments to think or reflect, we take that time to berate ourselves. We spend that precious private time worrying about something negative that we should or shouldn't have done.

I'm going to offer you a simple and very effective two step exercise that will help you bounce up quickly whenever life pushes you down. It's much like the personal achievement inventory mentioned previously. The first step in this exercise is to find a quiet time and place to sit down and think. Then focus your thoughts on a list of your personal and business accomplishments. Think only about the good things that have happened to you and review the positive actions you took to make them happen.

Review some of the challenges you've faced in both your personal and business life. Now recount the actions you took to manage them, and the results of those actions. In particular try to recall situations that initially made you feel like your sky was falling. Situations when you had to wrestle with self-doubt, and self kindled fears, anxieties and stress. Recall how you overcame them and moved forward toward your goals and objectives. Finally recall how you felt about yourself as a result of what you accomplished. Don't hold back in your praise for yourself set your modesty aside on this one and let the superlatives out.

The second step is to write down a description of a problem or challenging situation you currently find yourself in. One you've been thinking a lot about or maybe even obsessing over. On one side of the sheet of paper write down a brief first person account of the situation or challenge. Then turn the paper over and thinking back, list the steps you took to manage a similar one. Review again in your mind and then write down the reasons you chose the course of action you did. The final step is to think about and write out what you learned from the experience and how you can apply that knowledge to the current challenge you face. Use this simple method of reviewing and celebrating your positive achievements as a confidence booster whenever you start feeling like you're road kill on the highway of negativity. Remember, sometimes we get so busy fighting the good fight that we forget to remind ourselves of the good fights we've fought and won.

My wife will willingly attest to the fact that I'm not good at fixing things around the house. In fact saying I'm not good at fixing things is like saying the Titanic had a little problem with ice. I'm a full-fledged disaster around the house. My ineptitude with the tool belt over the years has led me to convince myself that I am not competent mechanically and so I have no confidence in my ability to perform even the most rudimentary household repairs. Now the cynics among you may say this is all a plot designed to free me up to play more golf. Shame on you for being skeptical, doubting my sincerity and making fun of the mechanically challenged. It has slowly dawned on me through years of trial and error, crooked shelves and near electrocutions that only when you feel competent while doing something, will you develop the confidence to take on the challenge of doing it.

Our personal motivations can spring from any number of sources and our desire to improve our competence in any aspect of our lives can be driven by any number of reasons. Most of us can be motivated by external influences or take the necessary steps to motivate ourselves because of our belief that improved competence will lead to improved performance which in turn will lead to better results and the accompanying rewards. It might lead to better and more satisfying inter-personal relationships, or it could lead to better on the job performance resulting in additional income or job promotion. If you believe as I do, that when your competence increases, so does your confidence, then you will also appreciate that the more confident you are the more willing you will be to take on the challenge and make the effort to improve your competence.

In your chosen field of professional sales it is absolutely essential to your success that you make an effort to learn as much about the skills of your profession as you can. In your profession there are proven methods of communicating with your customers, conducting a sales presentation and closing a sale to name a few that are time tested and results proven. You need to take the time to learn to become a competent salesperson before you start inflicting yourself on poor unsuspecting potential or existing customers.

Your profession is a perfect example of one where the blending of competence and confidence is essential to long-term success. You need to develop and maintain a level of competence that will enable you to close more selling opportunities and lessen the likelihood of missed sales. It's really pretty simple, the more sales you make the fewer rejections you encounter the less frustration you suffer. The result of all this will be the increased self-confidence you need to move forward and take on the challenges that create additional selling opportunities.

Don't wait for others, applaud yourself Positive reinforcement is a proven motivator and confidence builder. So, why is it we are always so stingy with our positive reinforcement of ourselves. Most of us give ourselves a well-deserved pat on the back for a job well done about as often as the Grinch gives out Christmas presents. We are much quicker to compliment and reward those around us than we are to do the same for ourselves. We need to lighten up a little, shake ourselves out of our self-defined code of straight-jacket conduct and celebrate the good we do and the things we accomplish. Lift your nose off the stone once in awhile. If you're going to take the blame when there's a drought, take some of the credit when it rains. Micro-business entrepreneurs tell me one of the great differences between working with a team of colleagues in a large organization and being on their own is the lack of positive reinforcement they receive for a job well done. They miss the applause. There's nobody there to tell them what a great job they did, or leave a note telling them how much their efforts where appreciated.

When you work as part of a sales team you enjoy and appreciate getting positive reinforcement from outside sources like colleagues and sales managers. It's great to bask in the adoration of those around you who appreciate your accomplishments. But don't always only let others be the sole arbiters of which of your deeds should be recognized. Get in the habit of applauding yourself and rewarding yourself for jobs well done. What has this got to do with building self-confidence you might ask? It has a lot to do with it. When you recognize without undue modesty the pivotal role you play in your own success and you take responsibility for your part in that success you take a step in building your self-concept which contributes to the health and well-being of your self-confidence.

The level of our self-concept is in part determined by the degree of belief we have in ourselves and driven by the respect we have for ourselves. Our self-concept is a measure of how much we respect, appreciate and enjoy being who we are. Everybody loves a winner so make sure you take steps to consistently remind yourself that you're a winner and reward yourself for your wins. We've all found ourselves in situations when we've had to overcome a challenge through perseverance, or creativity and we just wouldn't give in to the circumstances. Each time we see a situation like that through to a positive conclusion we need to recognize and reward the person who made the effort to make it happen. That person more often than not will be you. Some self-doubt can be healthy. The only people I know who are never down, always positive about everything and never bothered by anything are usually heavily sedated and found in institutions. Yes, you want to be positive and you want to develop your self-confidence, but you are also a thinking intelligent realist. You understand that occasionally you are going to find yourself in situations and surrounded by circumstances that will test both your positive resolve and self-confidence and create self-doubt.

This is only natural for anyone who chooses to break free of what is and seek out the new possibilities challenges and opportunities of what could be. When we decide to take risks, even before we take the first step forward we usually encounter that little nagging voice in our heads called self-doubt. We know only those who are prepared to risk failure can ever hope to achieve, but that fact doesn't make the decision to move out of our comfort zone any easier or less fraught with worry or self-doubt. Anytime we chart a new course and prepare to sail unfamiliar waters the realist in us will throughout the process question why we have chosen to do it, while the idealist in us urges us on. The key to keeping self-doubt and self-confidence in balance is to respect the reality of the situation but don't let in dampen the dream. Accept the fact that some self-doubt is part of the price you're going to pay when you challenge yourself, respect it but don't give in to it.

My suggestion is, that you don't waste your time and energy trying to figure out ways to overcome or block out doubts that are bound to enter the thoughts of anyone who bothers to think before they take action. Instead, use your self-doubt to your advantage; make it part of your decision making filtering system. Use it as a barometer to test not only your resolve, but also your flexibility. Face your doubts head on and instead of letting them overwhelm you learn to manage them and take advantage of them, while still being wary of them.

Sometimes its best to heed them and move forward with caution, or take a new direction. There are many paths you can take that will lead you toward your destination. Even the most committed among us, will find forks in the road. Self-doubt is sometimes an early warning signal to re-think what we are doing or the path we are following. Remember though, having respect for self-doubt doesn't mean giving in to it, every time you encounter it. The key to using it to your advantage is to continue to move forward but look for possible alternatives to the path you've chosen or the actions you're taking. Only when you stop moving toward or retreat completely from your objectives will you have given in to your self-doubt.

The most fertile ground for growing self-doubt and imagined fears is inactivity. It's fear of what might be, and the imagined consequences of actions taken that causes us to seek the safety of do nothing inactivity. It becomes another circle of self-defeat, limiting your potential by limiting your resolve to take action. I believe the best way to put a positive spin on self-doubt and minimize its' negative impact and debilitating effects on you is to recognize that only when we are striving to make a difference in our lives will we encounter it. Surely, a little self-doubt is a manageable price to pay to fulfill the promise that lies within us. I think it goes without saying that none of us make the right decisions all of the time, every time. It's when we let down our guard and let ourselves focus too much of our attention on looking back to the mistakes we've made instead of ahead to the opportunities we have that we lose our perspective on self-doubt. Go ahead make your decisions and get on with your actions secure in the knowledge that you've done your best.

Appreciate and enjoy who you are and what you do. The people who are the most fun to be around are those who are self-confident enough to enjoy being who they are, and doing what they do. Self-confidence is contagious and those people are carriers. We've all had the experience of spending time with someone and afterwards feeling better about ourselves and energized by the experience. Chances are we were caught in the reflection of their self-confidence and that's why we enjoyed and gained from the experience.

People with a competitive nature, when embarking on a selling career often put undo pressure on themselves to succeed as quickly as possible. Pressure can also be brought by the need to prove themselves to their peers or sometimes because of management dictates. Sometimes it's a financial squeeze that causes pressure to generate immediate results. It would be nice if we could all just make up our minds to burst out of the starting blocks in our race to success and start generating immediate sales results. However, the reality in most cases is, mutually beneficial business relationships take time to nurture and jell. At the beginning of your career, having confidence in yourself and enjoying what you do can provide you with much needed breathing space. Self-confidence can help you learn to have patience and work in harmony with your job. It helps you allow yourself time to grow into it and give your skills time to improve.

Almost every business has a rhythm to it and most have seasonal cycles. The business I'm in always slows down in the summer months. Companies hold fewer conferences and so speakers are in less demand. For the first few years when I was new to the speaking circuit I lacked the confidence to work in harmony with it. I would always try to force the market when it wasn't there. Instead of using the time to improve my skills or gain additional knowledge, or just plain take some down time. Not being real quick it took me a few years to learn to slow down when the market wanted to, and relax my pace when my customers did. There is seldom any upside to searching desperately for ways to increase your workload when your customers are tying just as desperately to lighten theirs. In my case the result of working against instead of with the rhythm of my customers was a lot of wasted effort, energy and financial resources. Not to mention the blows to my at the time fragile self-confidence. It also meant that when my customers ramped up at the end of their summer siestas, rejuvenated and ready to throw themselves back into the usual pace of business I was tired physically mentally and emotionally. I was out of step with my market, my business and myself. It was only after I learned to have the confidence to adjust to the rhythm of the market that I began to enjoy what I did and found more success in doing it.

When you develop the confidence to work in harmony with your market sector you find yourself swimming with instead of against the current. As a sales professional you will find yourself being more in control of what you can control and more tolerant of and patient with what you can't. When I began my business it took control of me in subtle ways. I found myself always thinking about and focusing on what I was planning to and hoping to accomplish tomorrow while looking over my shoulder and reviewing what I should have or could have done better yesterday. What it robbed me of was any chance I had to enjoy what I was doing while doing it. With an increase in confidence came a change in the way I thought of things, and the way I did things. I was less willing to live in the future or the past and let the present slip by unnoticed and unappreciated. I was still driven to accomplish all that I could but I began to be more appreciative of what I was accomplishing. I began getting more enjoyment out of myself and what I was doing. Sales professionals eventually come to realize they are the window through which their customers see their products or services. Often times in the minds of your customers you are the business. You have to learn to enjoy and appreciate who you are and what you do before your customers can see into it and pick up on it.

Chapter Sixteen
Become a New Opportunity Seeker

To escape risk, do nothing, say nothing and be nothing.

Selling is a risky business and the life of a professional sales practitioner certainly comes with its fair share of risk. A friend of mine who has been one of the top producing salespeople in his company for over twenty years believes the world is made up of only two types of people, risk avoiders, and risk takers.

I don't see it quite that simply. Anyone in the main stream of business is of course constantly faced with choices. Most if not all of which involve seeking opportunity and moving ahead by accepting some risk or staying put by either seeking to avoid it or choosing not to accept it when confronted by it. So I divide people into what I call status quo protectors and new opportunity seekers. Status quo protectors are content to build and protect their comfort zone bunkers.

Why take chances when I've always managed to get by on what's always worked in the past, is how they most often respond to new thoughts, ideas and ways of doing things. Whenever an opportunity presents itself along with some degree of accompanying risk their first reaction is to flee to the bunker to think and analyze the risk versus reward potential. They carefully weigh the risk in taking new or different actions and playing to win, versus the safety of doing it the old way, holding on to what they have and avoiding any potential loss. Status quo protectors are always content to settle for what they can safely have instead of seizing an opportunity to go for what they might be able to get. They settle for what is, primarily to avoid the possibility of failure or rejection. Failure or rejection being the two factors opportunity seekers must face in order to move forward and seize opportunity. No doubt by settling, status quo protectors lessen stress, remove pressure and avoid the possibility of having to deal with short or long term failure. But comfort zone bunkering also means convincing themselves that what they have is what they want, no more no less. They are content to have what they have and play it safe. No self-driven demands, no self-driven ambition, for status quo protectors, those types of things might upset their current state of being and result in frustration or dissatisfaction with what is.

Professional sales practitioners must be new opportunity seekers. New opportunity seekers understand and are comfortable with risk. They understand that in most life changing or life style enhancing situations greater risks offer greater rewards. Successful sales practitioners are people who are willing to admit they want more out of life, and are willing to go for it. They demand more from themselves and more importantly are willing to take the risks that are a part of moving forward in life and growing as a person. As soon as you take the first step of admitting to yourself you want more of what there is to have, you immediately shake up your own status quo. There is almost always some degree of putting in jeopardy what you do have, when you decide to take action and go after what you could have. This creates tension between the need to feel safe doing what you've always done and what you are most comfortable doing versus the desire to accept the risk, move forward and experience new ways of doing. Everyone no matter how self confident and secure feels twinges of doubt when taking on new ventures. But the alternative is to settle for less than you are capable of being and less than you are capable of having.

Every sales practitioner is always on the hunt for new opportunities and searching for increased ways of generating business. The world of professional sales is one in which the most successful people are the ones able to consistently generate selling opportunities. You can only do that by combining positive thoughts with constructive actions. Like most things in life, the opportunities to succeed also hold the potential to fail.

I entered the world of professional sales in the life insurance sector many years ago and it was a real eye opener for a young 24 year old who other than clerking part-time in a store while attending school, had never sold anything to anyone. In those years we were taught one sure fire way to get business was to contact all of our acquaintances, friends and relatives and in addition make telephone cold calls to the rest of the inhabitants of the known world. Well, first off just let me say that I apparently have a family and group of friends who are great believers in life insurance so much so that everyone of them had all they needed. It's hard enough to face rejection from people you don't know let alone those you do.

The only way for me to build a customer base was to contact people I didn't know and offer them my product, and the way to do that was to make prospecting cold calls. The level of sophistication in those days left a little to be desired. There were no demographic breakdowns of potential customers or pre-qualified lists of prospects. The system we employed for uncovering potential new clients began when the branch manager handed each of us rookie salespeople a phone book and told us it was our book of sales leads. It was 1970 and telephone solicitation was in its' infancy. It was prior to the onslaught of telephone marketers who have made it an art form to call you and me at the most inopportune time imaginable to try to sell us whatever it is we don't need. However the rejection to appointment ratio for most of us still hovered around the ninety-seven percent mark, meaning for every hundred calls we could probably generate three leads. What that also meant was that for every one hundred calls we made, we faced being rejected about ninety-seven times. We were of course armed with a canned sales pitch the training director had assured us was tried and true and delivered results. It took about 20 minutes of real world phoning to destroy whatever confidence had been built up in two weeks of training. The whole process was one of sink or swim.

I've been around salespeople most of my life and I know very few of them who jump out of bed first thing in the morning yelling, thank you God for another day to do more cold call prospecting. There's a price to be paid for success in any field the price salespeople pay is prospecting for new business leads. When all or part of your income is based on selling performance you quickly learn that sales results are a combination of two factors. First is your ability to create opportunities. The only way most of us can do that is to prospect for new business by contacting potential customers we are not currently doing business with or prospect for additional business with the customers we currently do have.

The second factor is how consistently we are able to convert the opportunities we create, into the sales that generate income. It quickly becomes obvious to anyone who has participated in any selling process that the first part of the process is rife with opportunity for prospecting anxiety to raise its' ugly head and the second part of the process is a breeding ground for sales presentation rejection. However, anyone who has made their living, as a sales professional will tell you that consistent prospecting for new customers and consistent prospecting for additional selling opportunities with existing customers is the only way to sustain long term success and earn an above average level of income. That still doesn't lessen the fact that for most of us the act of having to call total strangers and make our sales pitch to them can cause night sweats and morning heaves.

The keys to any productive prospecting system are; first develop one you are comfortable working with, second make sure it generates consistent results and third have a system for evaluating your efforts. Most failures occur when sales-people fail to heed the latter two keys. They don't prospect for business consistently enough and they don't evaluate the results they are getting and figure out what is working for them and what isn't. When you don't measure the results of your efforts, you'll be like the blind pig that occasionally finds an acorn, cause for celebration when it happens, but hardly a process designed to generate consistent results. You can't afford to stumble blindly about in search of business. You've got to know what works for you and what doesn't.

One of the most unproductive and personally damaging things any of us can do with any facet of our lives is to blindly continue doing what isn't working for us and hope somehow sometime the results might change. The first time I traveled to Europe as a tourist I was completely unprepared for the fact that few people outside the big cities spoke even rudimentary English. I had made an effort to learn some basic phrases in other languages but being able to say good morning my name is, doesn't mean much when you're desperate to find a washroom. I fell into the laughable trap of believing that when you encounter someone who doesn't speak your native tongue the best thing to do is speak more slowly and when that doesn't work try a combination of slow and loud. Obviously I wasted a lot of people's time and tested their patience by trying to communicate with them using a system that simply wasn't working. It didn't matter how slowly I spoke, or how loudly I yelled, the problem was the language I was using was the wrong one. I tried speaking to a lot of people but the results weren't there. I was putting in the effort but the language I was using kept me from being successful in communicating with the people I was trying to talk to. The result was one very frustrated tourist and I'm sure more that a few puzzled Europeans. You need to evaluate your prospecting efforts as you go and adjust them to the circumstances you find yourself in well before your frustration level causes you to give up and stop making the effort.

The only reason I can think of for any semi-sane sales professional to put themselves through the agonies of sales prospecting is to generate opportunities to get them in front of a decision maker and make their sales presentation. The good news is that once you have secured an opportunity to make a presentation there is no great mystery to making it. The purpose of this book is not to get into the minute details of how to make an effective sales presentation. There are more than a few books on the market that can take you through that process. I would like to share just this one thought with you on how to present yourself in the best possible light. I've found over the years, the most fool-proof way to present myself in any sales situation was to imagine I was a guest in someone's home for the first time, and conduct myself accordingly.

It's a simple, easy to understand and apply way of presenting yourself and your product or service in a positive light. If you were visiting with the customer in their home for the first time. I think you would make an effort to engage them in conversations that focused on topics of interest to them. You would probably touch on relevant situations, circumstances and issues they faced. You would have a conversation not conduct an interrogation. You would compare and share information through non–threatening conversational questions and comments. I believe when you follow those simple guidelines and structure your sales presentation accordingly you will improve your results.

The old, "if I've got it, you need it" high pressure selling of the past will not work with today's more educated and sophisticated buyers. Today's sales practitioners are hard working, creative professionals. They know the value and pay-off of putting the needs of their customers first. The buying experience for most of us is enjoyable. What we don't enjoy or appreciate is the having someone trying to sell us something we don't want or need. I don't and I'm sure you don't, enjoy being subjected to high pressure selling tactics. When most of us set out to make a significant purchase, what we want is the opportunity to make an informed buying decision. We like to make our decision to buy with the help of an informed, helpful, empathetic and energetic salesperson. Your customers and prospects deserve and expect the same. They are more likely to buy from you when you put their needs and interests first. Loyalty, repeat business and referrals are some of the rewards associated with this customer first style of selling.

Work at positioning yourself within your target market. In order to produce consistent sales results any selling process must include a sales presentation that enables the salesperson to get to the heart of the customer's needs and offer workable solutions. There is another element of the process that is too often ignored and little understood. It addresses the importance to the salesperson of being able to identify qualified prospects within their target market sector. Struggling salespeople too often try to play the pure numbers game. They keep themselves busy trying to sell their products or services to suspects instead of investing the time and effort to uncover qualified prospects. The financial services sector offers a good example. There is no point in financial planners having a sales presentation that pin points the needs of potential clients and outlines the benefits of doing business with them, without also knowing how to find potential clients with the where-with-all to take advantage of what is being offered. Having the worlds best selling process including a dynamic sales presentation isn't going to generate results until and unless the salesperson is able to deliver the presentation to the right people, in the right way at the right time. Every successful sales process begins with the salesperson's ability to uncover a prospect / customer need, or create a prospect / customer want. The process culminates when the salesperson is successful in convincing a qualified prospect or customer to take action, take the action with them and take it now.

A word here about competition. In the highly competitive world of professional sales, you need to be ready to compete, but also recognize that there can be more than one winner. Accept the fact that you will face other highly motivated and skilled competitors. Don't focus all of your thoughts and energies on how to compete with your competitors and lose track of how best to serve your customers. Work toward executing your way of doing things better than they do theirs.

Work on fine tuning and refining the way you offer your service or product to your prospects and always be looking for new ways to bring value to your existing customers. Never overestimate or underestimate your competition. Have respect for them, but don't drive yourself nuts worrying about what they do or how they do it. There are times to be pro-active and initiate your own new ideas and ways of doing things and there are times to be reactive and adopt, adapt and replicate the successful strategies of your competitors and make them your own. Our old nemesis anxiety manifests itself in all kinds of different ways. It can cause you to fear your competition and it can lower your self-confidence. Have you ever taken part in a game of golf, or cards or chess and because you feared your opponent's ability you focused too much on beating him or her instead of on winning the game? It is of course always wise to respect your competitors, but it is never to your advantage to fear them.

Anxiety and at its worst can turn healthy respect for your competitors into an unhealthy fear of them. This is especially true for people just entering the selling game. I know in the early years of my career when I knew the customer was inviting both me and three or four of my competitors to make presentations and I knew I was going up against someone with a lot more experience, I had a tendency to feel anxious and fearful about my chances. It would throw me off my game plan. I would be too focused on trying to counter what I thought my competitors were going to offer and not focused enough on what my product could do for the customer. Instead of selling on my strengths I was counter selling against the strengths of my competitors. It took me a while but I finally figured it out. It had as much to do with my self-confidence as it did my sales ability.

I began to take a detailed look at my product as seen through the eyes of my customers. I found the more I began to appreciate the quality of the product I was selling and the more I believed in the benefits it could provide to my customers the more confident I became and the more sales I made. If your confidence is down a quart and you have doubts about the product or service you are selling, you are in a lose-lose situation and my advice would be to find something to sell that you can believe in.

If on the other hand, your confidence is down but you are selling a quality product or service, put the onus on what you're selling to carry the day. So what if you're up against people you feel are better salespeople, or have more experience. If you are one hundred percent convinced that what you are selling can and will benefit your prospects or customers, you have an obligation to get it in front of them and give them an opportunity to purchase it. Your confidence in your product will eventually make you a more confident seller of it. Another way to overcome competitor fear is through knowledge. Make sure you are staying on top of what is going on in your market sector, find out just what your competitors are offering and how it stacks up against what you have. That way your customers can count on you as a knowledgeable advisor not just a push the product salesperson.

I don't think its possible to rise above being average at what you do until you really start believing in who you are, what you do, and how you do it. It's very difficult if not impossible to overcome severe fear of rejection or prospecting anxiety without believing in all three.

Chapter Seventeen
Combining Values and Leadership

The time you spend thinking of ways to impress people, would be better spent doing things they are likely to be impressed by.

Is leadership overrated, maybe it is, maybe it isn't. Certainly when we think of leadership we too often think of people with influence or power. Or we probably think of politicians, business managers, or maybe coaches and athletes. These are all people who hold positions of prominence but they may or may not be leaders. Part of leading others is to accept the responsibility to inspire them to do things, do them well and want to do more of them because they share a common goal and most importantly want to.

Leading others does have its limitations when it comes to the results it can generate. You can be a terrific leader but if you don't have the support of the people you're leading or they lack the knowledge, skill and expertise necessary to do the job you and they aren't going to achieve much. You see examples of this in team sports all the time. A team wins and the coach is lauded for his or her great leadership, coaching expertise and motivational skills. Then when the supporting cast of players on the team changes and the level of their collective talent and skills drops and they begin to lose, everyone questions the leadership, coaching and motivational capabilities of the coach. A coach with good leadership skills can take a group of skilled players and raise the level of their performance, but he or she can't raise the dead. If the people playing for them are underachieving because they lack the skills needed to raise the level of their performance, leadership isn't going to have much impact until the root problem of skills development is addressed. Enthusiastic, optimistic and positive leadership can make others raise the level of their commitment to trying, but without knowledge, skills and talent it won't make them successful.

Self–leadership puts the onus of leading squarely where it belongs, on the individual. Instead of waiting to follow someone else's lead you lead the way for yourself. You don't wait for someone else to set your agenda you take the initiative to set it yourself. I don't mean you don't play on the team and play by the rules. What I'm suggesting is, when you're self-led you don't wait for others to challenge you. You challenge yourself and you set your own higher than demanded personal performance standards.

Every leader is first and foremost a dealer in hope. You have to work at creating a positive image of a preferred future one that embraces what you hope to achieve. Then you have to make it easy to buy into the possibility of that future by defining the manageable steps you will take to get there. In order to make any lasting changes to the way you think or the way you act, you first have to build an image of what you could have that is better than what you do have. Most people have an image of their future tucked somewhere in the recesses of their minds. If that image is of an average future their performance will reflect it. If the image you have of your future is filled with the rewards of success, your actions will be guided by that image. Our determination to succeed and the actions that accompany that determination are influenced by our expectations. The expectations we have of ourselves set the tone and pace of the actions we take and the quality of our thoughts. Which in turn determine the level of success we are likely to achieve.

Your determination to become self-led will be driven in large measure by your commitment to your personal values. Your personal values reflect your dedication to things like caring, pride, honesty, and integrity. They are built on the things you believe in, stand for and are willing to stand up for. They are the intangible things that contribute to the way your customers feel about you and what make them comfortable doing business with you. Personal values are what we bring to relationships.

Your self-leadership like a lot of other things is put to the true test when it's time to take action. It shows up when you decide to take on a challenge that others shy away from. It shows up when you decide to do something, while others conclude there is nothing to be done. It gives you the courage to get involved when others are content to stand back waiting, hoping and watching. We've all had more than our fair share of 'those days'. Those days when nothing we do seems to go right. The point is, no matter how positive you are, or how much you may have your act together, there are going to be things happening everyday around you and to you that you can't foresee but you have to react to. It's your reactions to unforeseen and unplanned situations that really test your self-leadership and personal values. Without a strong foundation of personal values your reactions to out of your control situations and circumstances is often destructively emotional. Fly-off-the-handle, negative reactions are what can cause simple problems to escalate into full-blown catastrophes.

Personal values and self-leadership free you to look confidently into your future and make decisions designed to give you some control over it. It doesn't matter where you work or who you work for, even if it's yourself none of us is ever totally in control of our little corner of the world all of the time. The world around us and the market sector we are employed in have their own ongoing dynamics that no one person controls. We can however put ourselves in a position to gain more control than most when our thoughts and actions are guided by self-leadership and positive personal values. We are less likely to be as reactionary to the influences around us. We are more likely to stick to the path that we've chosen and much less likely to get caught up in endlessly wandering and drifting in search of immediate gratification.

Personal values combined with self-leadership become your internal global tracking system they guide you to the future you want to have while helping you take the right turns and avoid the wrong ones. Along the journey it's your personal values that send signals to other people making them aware of what you believe in, and what you are willing to stand up for. In the fast paced and ever changing world of professional sales a simple personal value like standing by your word, is a powerful influence on your customers, one that is likely to generate repeat and referral business.

There are many unspoken benefits associated with conducting your business in accordance with strong personal values, two of which always pay long term dividends. The first is, they help your customers feel secure and comfortable doing business with you. Over time they come to understand and appreciate that with you, what they see, is what they get. The second is, they make you feel more comfortable and confident with the way you do business. A strong commitment to positive personal values keeps you on the right path, when you encounter life's forks in the road. Our values are what help give us the energy and will to move forward and over those rough stretches of road we all encounter from time to time.

Our personal values encourage us to do our best and do what's right even when there's no one there to notice. They encourage us to think in terms of what's right, not just what's right for us. Personal values that exemplify who we are and what we believe in make it easier to reach our objectives. They help simplify the all too complicated world we live in and bring order to the chaos that surrounds us. They give us a sense of purpose. Personal values keep our self-leadership on track by helping us prioritize what we should be doing and how best to get it done. The result is, we ultimately accomplish more in less time, with less stress.

You accomplish more in less time because you are working at your own self-determined level of performance. You encounter less stress because when you are self-led you learn to believe in and trust your own abilities. Less stress always equals more drive and determination to compete and win. Over time instead of hoping for success, you come to expect it.

When you commit to your personal values and practice self-leadership you find yourself better able to break free from the bonds of what you used to be and able to enjoy more fully the freedom to become what you would like to be. If you have simply been a cog in the machine for five or ten or even twenty years you are very likely to see yourself in terms of what you do, instead of who you are. Self-leadership enables and encourages you to look through what you've been doing to what you could be doing. Then it can guide you through the process of taking the constructive actions needed to put you in a position to do it. Professional sales practitioners will find self-leadership essential in helping raise the level of their performance. You will find yourself demanding more productivity from your actions not just to meet sales targets or quarterly quotas but because you are less accepting of being average and just getting by.

The road we all travel is seldom free of potholes. Commitment to your personal values and the determination to be self-led can help smooth your ride but it doesn't mean you aren't going to run into some rough stretches. You're still going to question yourself along the way. You're still going to have times when you mumble and grumble to yourself about what you should have done or did or didn't do. The strength of your convictions is always being tested and for that reason your personal values had better be clear to you. They are the unseen things that affect and impact on your ability to stay true to yourself. Things like caring about how your actions affect you and the people around you. Taking pride in what you accomplish and who you've become and balancing it with enough humility to still get your head through the door. Being honest with yourself and in your dealings with people, even when the result may not be what it could be if you weren't. Being reliable so that you know what to expect from yourself on the average days that make up most of our lives. Having a sense of humor and knowing when and how to laugh at yourself and when not to laugh at others. A simple thing like standing by your word is a personal value that has more potential to affect the way you live your life and conduct your business than any ten-page written guarantee with enough small print to dazzle a corporate lawyer ever will.

Those are all personal values that are easy to think about, and talk about but not so easy to practice. Self-leadership and personal values work in tandem each giving you the strength of character to commit to the other. Personal values help you stay true to yourself and your core beliefs. They contribute to helping you be the type of person who does what's right simply because it's the right thing to do. They help you be the person who takes the right actions even when there's no one there to judge. Self-leadership helps you live your life, run your business and deal with people on a very simple premise. That premise is this; that beyond the written law there is a much more powerful one with a much greater influence on encouraging us to do what's right, that is the law of human decency.

How often is it that we see a wide variation between what people say they are and what their actions show they are. Actions still speak louder than words. To say that people get what they deserve is wrong in some cases but right in most. People with no sense of self-leadership and no values to guide them tend to find themselves drifting through life being pushed and pulled by the prevailing thoughts and actions of those around them. They are almost certainly destined to run into other like-minded people, content to take what comes and hope for the best. Is it any wonder then that their predisposition to fail becomes a self-fulfilling prophesy.

At the other end of the spectrum, when our drive and determination is fueled by personal values we will almost certainly find ourselves in the company of others with the same high degree of determination to think and act in accordance with what it takes to reach their goals and objectives. The idea that 'like attracts like' kicks in. We see this all the time. We surround ourselves with people who share similar values, ideals and philosophies. We like people like us.

We sometimes have to make the tough decision to see less of some old friends and more of new ones as our values change. Most of us like to hold on to long-term friendships from bygone days. But sometimes the parameters of those friendships change. Some of our longtime friends who change their priorities and refocus their energies in similar ways to us, we see more of. Others who never made the commitment to adjusting their values to reflect new responsibilities we see less of.

Sometimes we reach points in our lives when our values are put to the test and they put us in direct conflict with friends and family. What we may see as an attempt to break free from old restrictive thoughts and unproductive behaviors that are now in direct conflict with our new lifestyle, career goals and objectives, they may see as an attempt to be better than them, set ourselves apart and sell out. When this happens we may even find ourselves the target of ridicule, contempt or even hostility from close friends and family. When new values and determinations require you to think and act differently people around you locked into the same old, same old, are going to be uncomfortable with the new and different you. It's at that point that you have to rely on your newly adopted self-leadership and personal values to guide you.

I went through a situation like I'm describing early in my adult life. I grew up in a blue-collar city dominated by heavy industry. I grew up in a family of four boys. My mother was a stay at home housewife and my father was employed in a middle-income job. I grew up in an environment I would describe today as average for the times and the place. My parent's limited social life was spent with friends attending house parties. Card parties and lots of social drinking rounded out their social activities. The expectation was that my brothers and I would follow in my parent's footsteps. Find similar middle class jobs and participate in a similar lifestyle. For a while it seemed each of us would fulfill this somewhat limited destiny. My first full time job after high school was at one of the steel companies and in those years I fit right in. My social life revolved around family and friends who I had gone to school with and who were working in similar jobs, living similar lifestyles. A few years later I decided that I wanted something more from life and began to develop a new outlook and different more productive and positive set of values. In a very short time I was in conflict with some of my family and friends. I had to let go of some of the friendships that had been the bedrock of my adolescent life.

I even went through some turbulent years with members of my family. In looking back I am now convinced they were waiting for this strange phase of my life to end. They were convinced that sooner or later I would return to what they considered to be the life style to which I, and they were entitled. My brothers remained true to their upbringing, I moved on. If there is a point to this story it's this. When you set out to change through the development of new values you risk alienating the people who are comfortable with the old you. When you establish new more challenging goals and objectives that can only be reached by developing a different mindset and more productive behaviors you are also going to find new places to be, things to do, and people to be with. The people who were most comfortable with the old you, and are skeptical or resentful of what you're trying to become will stay where they are and fill the void you leave with people who think and act like they do.

When you make a conscious decision to become self-led and begin using your personal values to guide and direct your thoughts and behaviors you begin to understand the limitations of the options you had without them. When you begin to think more positively and act more productively you begin to understand how to avoid being victimized by the negative thoughts and actions of people around you.

You can only begin to move out of what is now and into what could be in the future by doing two things. First you need to start building up your self-concept so that you can begin to think more positively and constructively about the person you are and what you are capable of accomplishing. You need to have an unwavering belief in yourself before you can make a commitment to risking what you have to get what you want. Then you have to instill in yourself a tenacious determination to start thinking about putting yourself in situations and places that will bring you into touch with the kind of people who can help you become the person you want to be.

Almost every day you make decisions about how to invest your time. There are other days when you don't have a choice of investing it at all. You have to spend it doing things that need doing and are not in your direct control. In spite of those days, you do have a surprising number of days when you can make a conscious decision on who you want to invest your time with and what you want to invest it doing. It's your self-leadership and values that determine the choice of where and with whom you choose to invest the time that's yours. Without them, you're bound to waste one of your most precious commodities.

Your personal values impact on your actions by influencing your thoughts. It's your actions you use to bring your plans thoughts and ideas together in order to make something positive happen. It's like the difference between studying all of the theories and watching all of the tapes about how to groove your golf swing and actually stepping up to the tee and hitting the ball. The proof is always in the doing.

You can use a combination of your thoughts and actions to push back the limits of your limitations. You can make use of self-leadership to consistently build your self-confidence. You can also put it to use by confronting and besting new challenges and seeing yourself as a winner. We all have a need to feel good about ourselves, be happy with who we are and be valued and respected by people around us. When we feel good about ourselves we are energized to go out and make productive things happen. When we hold ourselves in high esteem others tend to do the same and that mutual respect can be the basis of valuable and lasting business relationships and personal friendships.

Chapter Eighteen
Put Your Positive Attitude to Work

The real secret to success is finding something you love to do and then finding a way to convince others to pay you to do it.

So you're one of those motivational speakers, I hear that comment all the time when I'm introduced to people. Yes, I am a speaker who talks about positive motivation, I always reply. I then go on to say; but no one outside influence can truly make a lasting motivational impact on you, until you decide you want to be motivated. I can act as a guide to point out the benefits of positive motivation or suggest ways and means of finding the motivation you want. It has to be you though who decides who will motivate you, what will motivate you and when you are ready to be motivated. Please don't mistake long term, sustainable and personally beneficial motivating influences for the quick fix 30 minute shot of motivational energy you get from listening to speakers like me. It's great fun to be at an event where a good speaker gets you turned on and cranked up while listening to his or her message. If it weren't I would probably have to go out and find honest work. That kind of motivational impact is like drinking a double espresso with extra sugar. It'll give you a quick caffeine and sugar high, but it won't last long. You are the only one who can truly decide how you are going to motivate yourself and what you are going to use to do it. Some people use their faith in themselves, others use spiritual faith to motivate and guide them, some use well defined goals and objectives, some rely on family to motivate them, some if truth be told are motivated by fear.

The real power and impact of whatever influence you use to create and sustain your personal motivation can be measured in its capacity to cause you to take positive actions. I remember having a conversation with a newly appointed sales manager for a large farm equipment manufacturer. When I asked him what he though his greatest challenge was going to be, he responded quickly and confidently by saying; motivating my salespeople to sell more product is the real challenge as I see it. Well he got it partly right. He was just getting the cart before the horse. You can't motivate people to sell. What you can do is help them be motivated to take the kind of constructive actions that will lead to consistent selling opportunities. It's a combination of the number of actions they take and the quality of those actions that will result in increased sales. My friend the sales manager can help motivate his people by sharing his knowledge and with practical tips on how to stay the course and generate selling opportunities. He can help them mange their time so that it's used more efficiently.

But only when his salespeople find their personal motivation will they embrace his ideas and use them to improve the quality of their performance. In the end it's not just how often they take action that will generate increased results. It's also the quality of the actions they are taking that will ultimately increase their sales results. Motivation that comes from within us is what causes us to want to get better at what we do. Having to get better to meet some artificial outside demand may work in the short term, but the lasting willingness to make the sacrifices and make the effort to win can only be sustained from within. In the end it is always the quality of how we do what we do that impacts the most on how well we get it done. It's the power of our personal motivation that inspires the quality of our performance. It's ultimately what enables us to take on and overcome the challenges we face and generate the results we want. It's our personal motivation that also determines the level and quality of our attitude. Attitude can be either a shroud of pessimism and negativity we bury ourselves in, or it can be a cloak of optimism and hope we wrap ourselves in. It can be used as a catalyst to generate the motivation we need to take action and what motivates us to want to make sure the actions we take reflect the best of our ability. Even though in and of itself our attitude alone won't change the rules or outcome of the game.

The attitude we go into the game with will have a measurable effect on the way we play the game. Their outlook and attitude is what successful sales practitioners count on to produce the drive and determination needed to face their challenges, stick to their plan and create their opportunities. Because of their outlook and attitude they are also better able to recognize the face of opportunity when they see it. Don't look at developing an optimistic outlook and positive attitude only as the means to an end. Instead view them as integral parts of the process of getting there.

As one who preaches the advantages of optimistic outlook and positive attitude what I'm about to tell you next might be considered by some to be heresy and blasphemy. I believe the criteria for developing a strong personal positive attitude and outlook has nothing to do with being able to see a silver lining in every dark cloud. Park your rose tinted glasses somewhere else. This optimist looks at his world and sees the good, the bad and the ugly. It's our world warts and all, looking away isn't going to make them go away.

What concerns me most is that so much of what is written and talked about in reference to building and main-taining a positive attitude seems to ignore the reality of our everyday lives. The most productive positive thinkers are positive realists. They recognize the limits of their influence over situations and circumstances not of their own making. They believe in the golden rule of do unto others as you would have them do unto you. They also recognize that to some others it means, those with the gold make the rules. When your attitude is strong and healthy you find ways to be successful in the what - is of the here and now. You recognize the limits of your influence over others, and the need to work within the system. You don't have to like what you have to do, but you do have to do what you have to. This is not to say you don't try to bring your influence to bear, or thoughts and ideas to the table when and if you feel changes are needed. The important thing is you don't waste time railing against what is and undermining the system. You put your efforts into working toward what could be and improving what is. Positive thinking optimistic people aren't expecting to live and work in some Disneyesque fantasy world.

Stories about how positive thinking, positive faith or positive wishing turned hopeless situations into happy endings are very inspirational and do happen, but believing they are the norm instead of the exception can also be very misleading. It can leave people with the impression that attitude is the great dragon slayer that conquers all adversity. I believe that our attitude positive or negative in and of itself will always have a profound effect on what we do, how we do it, and the results we achieve. However, having the right attitude and outlook won't make any lasting significant impact on what we do until we decide to bring it to bear on the aspects of our lives that help us reach the success we're striving for. I know lots of people who are cheerful, optimistic and positive about everything, the only exception being while they are at work. They see work as something that has to be endured before the fun begins. They put in their time at work, but their effort at play. They're applying the magic of positive thinking to just one part of their lives and in so doing they rob themselves of the full impact it could have on their success. In the case of professional sales practitioners even as strong as the influences of having a positive attitude and optimistic outlook might be, they are not the singular ingredients needed in the success mix.

No matter how positive your attitude might be it won't achieve results on its own. Professional sales practitioners have to combine it with other ingredients like product knowledge, selling skills and constructive actions before it will have the anticipated impact on the results they are striving to achieve. There can be no question that in a sales driven environment a positive and productive attitude is essential to success. However, without accompanying skills and the talent to apply those skills correctly, it isn't going to generate consistently high results. A word of caution here, don't allow yourself to fall into the seductive trap of convincing yourself that positive attitude alone will bring you out of a sales slump. The simple fact is that it isn't the determination to continue to think positively that will do it. It's the resolve to continue to work constructively that will.

None of us gets very far by sitting back, blithely smiling and staying positive while the roof falls in around us. We aren't going to reach our potential by burying our heads in the sand, ignoring and wishing away potentially damaging, threatening and negative situations we encounter.

Working with a positive attitude means just that, working with it. It means being tuned into and aware of situations and challenges that are part of a productive life and using our positive attitude to respond to them with the energy and creativity that is called for.

Try thinking of positive attitude in these terms. A positive attitude is the reality-based belief that we can produce the results we seek. By applying a positive attitude to guide our constructive actions we give ourselves permission to use our knowledge, skills, time and efforts to reach out for what is ours for the taking.

Almost anyone still drawing a breath, is in a position to experience some moments of exhilaration, success or accomplishment no matter how small or seemingly insignificant. Those moments no matter how brief will inevitably produce some sense of personal well-being and contribute to at least a moment of positive attitude. Even the most cynical among us would have to admit, it's very difficult to experience negative winning, or negative accomplishment.

In my humble opinion winning sure beats the heck out of losing. When we use our positive outlook to help us increase our accomplishments we in turn feel better about ourselves. Those are great feelings to have, but there is a danger in becoming addicted to them. If you begin to rely only on accomplishments or wins to make you feel good about yourself and use them to maintain your outlook and attitude you set yourself up to ride an emotional roller coaster. When you rely strictly on results to measure your worth you develop a mind-set of winning isn't everything, it's the only thing. Instead of being in control you find yourself being controlled by the next rush that only winning can bring. The problem is, I'm yet to meet anyone who wins them all. It's wonderful to enjoy the highs associated with winning and accomplishing, but relying exclusively on success to feed your outlook and attitude is giving control of your feelings over to external and mostly uncontrollable forces.

A positive attitude is as hard to hold onto as a cold beer on a hot afternoon. That's why it has to be anchored by strong principles, beliefs, ideals and values. Things that we can control. Without a strong core commitment to our principles, beliefs, ideals and values it is difficult to stand firm against the persistent onslaught of negativity and pessimism that assaults us everyday.

Recently I was giving a talk to a business group in Toronto. I was the luncheon speaker so I had plenty of time to enjoy a leisurely room service breakfast and catch some of the morning television news shows. A report on the soon to open new eatons department stores caught my attention.

As I sat back to watch a panel of experts talk about the re-launch of the name and opening of the stores I was astounded and appalled at what I saw and heard. Every comment they made with few exceptions was couched in negativity. The marketing scheme was geared to the wrong clientele. The advertising didn't convey the right message and image. The stores were going to be too big. Management didn't understand what the new retailing was all about. They weren't going be able to provide the level of service they were promising. It began to become apparent to me that the members of the media and the experts on the panel, were completely unaware of the negative bias they were presenting. To them this was the window through which they viewed the world. There was no talk of the possible success of the new company and what might drive that success. There was no talk of the employment opportunities afforded to people. There was no talk of the possibility that some members of the purchasing public might like the marketing or advertising or might want to shop in the new stores. The entire exercise was one of negative one-upmanship. Too bad that these people had forgotten to remind themselves that any half-wit cynic can point out things that might go wrong, but it takes some work and some effort to analyze why things might go right.

One way to maintain a positive and productive attitude is to learn to lessen the link between judging yourself strictly by what you do or don't accomplish and begin judging yourself on the basis of how committed you are to being the kind of person you want to be. Your accomplishments should be important to you because they validate what you believe is the right way to do things not just because they bring you tangible rewards and recognition. Keep in mind that lasting success usually comes to those who feel good about what they do and how they do it. I don't mean you shouldn't enjoy the rewards of your efforts. I think most would agree with me when I say given the choice we'd rather be richer than poorer. My thought is simply this; when you are driven by your own unique spirituality which is the sum total of your combined principles beliefs, ideals, and values, you will not only enjoy the success you achieve, you'll also enjoy being the person who generates it. Rewards always go hand in hand with results. When you have a well-founded respect for yourself and for what you do you will always set your personal objectives higher than any arbitrary ones set for you by others. Your results always flow from your efforts. When your attitude frees you to focus on what your doing, instead of only on what you're going to get from doing it, the rewards will follow. Professional sales practitioners work in an uncompromising environment. Your successes and failures are constantly measured and analyzed. Your weekly, monthly, quarterly and yearly sales results are hung out to dry, for all to see. Yes yours is an uncompromising world of easily tallied wins and losses. When you judge yourself solely on what you do, without regard to who you are you risk becoming prone to measuring your success as a person exclusively in terms of the results of your efforts on the job. Steer clear of the temptation to let the positive level of your attitude and your corresponding self-worth and esteem rise and fall according to your latest sales figures. It's the old "what I do, is who I am" trap. More so than most you need to constantly remind yourself the sum of the parts makes up the whole. You need to work at measuring your success as a person by more than what you do or by the sales you do, or don't make. The most successful sales practitioners I've worked with have found a balance by placing equal emphasis on the person they are and the thing they do.

Am I born with my attitude or can I make my own? You build and adjust your attitude as you grow and develop as a person. I like to imagine that all of us are given a set of attitude building blocks at birth. The set we are given contains both positive and negative pieces. We have the choice as we grow and mature of which ones we use to build our attitude. When we are young children we are naturally optimistic and we like the positive pieces best.

We use those pieces to build with and as a result most of us begin with a solid foundation of positive pieces and a correspondingly open and positive attitude. This lasts pretty much until our teen-age years. It's then we begin to encounter heaping helpings of negative building blocks both real and imagined, some provided by our families or teachers or other authority figures in our lives but mostly offered to us by some of our peers. That's a natural part of the growing up process. The teen-age years are a time when feelings, emotions, thoughts, beliefs, values and faith crash together like shifting tectonic plates. Some resist the influences and impact of the negativity around them and continue to build with positive blocks. Others are swayed by the lure of cynicism and negativity and begin to replace their positive building blocks with negative ones. We move forward through our teenage years and into our adult working years.

At this point most of us have an attitude that is built on a mix of both positive and negative building blocks. Some with a preponderance of positive pieces, some leaning toward the negative. It's in the everyday working world that most of us have our most influential and memorable encounters with chronic negativity. We begin to encounter people who for various reasons have over the years thrown out their positive building blocks and replaced them with negatives. They have built an attitude constructed entirely of negative building blocks. These people pose a real threat to anyone with a positive attitude and optimistic outlook in two ways. First their negative attitude can wear you down. Second they are always more than willing to share their negativity with anyone they encounter. They have an amazing ability to locate extensive supplies of negative building blocks. They always have more than they need. They are always ready and willing to provide anyone around them with any extra negativity they might be looking for. It's about the time we encounter these negative people in real numbers that most of us become aware that we have a choice to make. Do we want to continue to look for the scarcer positive building blocks and continue to build our attitude with those, or do we take the easy way out. Start picking up the much more plentiful and easy to find negatives blocks and build with them.

Positive thinking drives productive actions. Have your thoughts about what might happen ever kept you from doing something you wanted to? How many times do we miss opportunities because we don't want to take a chance? How often won't we take chances because of the imagined negative results of our actions? Professional salespeople need to have a positive mind-set and be able to see in their minds-eye the positive results from taking chances. In terms of how you think and what you think about, you have to make an effort to visualize situations and circumstance in the positive. It's the only way you can consistently well up the courage you need to take the chances that often uncover new opportunities. Think for a moment about the impact your thoughts be they positive or negative have on your everyday actions. Let's say you're meeting friends tonight over dinner and drinks. Chances are you're going to be thinking positively about the night ahead and looking forward to all the great things that are going to happen. During the day you are your actions are likely to be productive because you're upbeat and thinking happy thoughts. On the other hand let's say you have a late day appointment with your dentist to have some oral surgery done. Chances are your mind-set is going to be negative and your thoughts filled with all the things that might go wrong. Your day will probably be less than productive because your distracted and thinking stressful thoughts.

Your thoughts program your course of action. They are a powerful stimulus and force. Your thoughts can and will contribute to your drive for success by positively influencing your attitude, behaviors and actions, or they will limit your potential by throwing up negative roadblocks.

Most of your days are filled with interactions and conversations with the people who make up your workday world, friends, co-workers, and customers. However and this may surprise you, the person you talk to most often, and most intimately to is yourself. Even during the most hectic of days, we are alone with ourselves and our thoughts a lot of the time. It's during these private talks with ourselves that we develop the blueprint we use to program our behaviors. It's during our self-talk that we weigh the pros and cons of actions we are considering taking.

I suspect that this scenario might be familiar to most of you. You are having a typically stress filled day. Can you relate yet? Someone or something does you an injustice. After the initial confrontation or scrimmage with the guilty party, you move on to other pressing matters. But all the while you are thinking negatively about what happened. You're replaying what went on complete with a lot of negative and self-pitying self-talk about how you were wronged. Your probably going to waste at least a little time thinking about the sweet revenge of getting even for the grievous injustice committed against you. Let me suggest that if you were able to have someone record your conversations and inter-action with other people for the next few hours you might be very surprised. Negative thinking always has a spill over effect, and it most often spills over on the innocent. People who had nothing to do with whatever it was that upset you become targets for your wrath. The negativity coursing through your veins needs a release and who better to dump on than the innocent and supportive.

No matter how positive we try to be, occasionally we are going to run into frustrating situations that test our resolve. My experience is that it is not the initial negative experience or situation that causes the most negative fall out. It's the actions we take following the incident and which are generated by the thoughts we are having about the incident that will cause the most damage. If we are unable to re-focus our thoughts on positive and productive ways to solve the problem or resolve the situation the negative fall out will continue.

There are ways to hasten your recovery, and get back on a positive track. The process begins with regaining control over your thoughts. Allow yourself a set period of time and give yourself complete freedom during that time to wallow in the negativity of the moment. I suggest 15 minutes tops for minor aggravations and up to 30 minutes for those real vein poppers. When your time is up, switch gears and start thinking and mentally talking to yourself about the kind of productive actions you can take to address the issue and solve the problem. Once you're back to being focused on positive thoughts, you are more likely to generate the positive energy you need to get on with positive actions.

We all have a choice concerning what we choose to fill the space between our ears with. We can fill it by taking a few minutes every morning to record a positive mind memo, to be played back throughout the day. Or, we can leave the space empty and let it be filled by whatever we encounter during the day, be it positive or negative. Lets face it, we've all had days when because of what's going on around us we get a little testy. Positive thoughts can drain away pretty quickly when we lose a sale or we face one of those days when every prospect we speak to seems to have a very limited vocabulary made up of, no, not interested, got enough, don't need it, don't want it, or don't ever darken my door again. It's days like those when our conversations with ourselves can easily turn negative. It's on days like those when we have to make a real conscious effort not to let negatives fill our cranial cavity.

Don't let your guard down and fall prey to any of the following common self-defeating negatives.

- I'm not smart enough to face the challenge.
- I'm too old to be starting over.
- This is just more of the same old, same old.
- They've already got their minds make up.
- What I do isn't going to make any difference.
- I might as well take some time off and think about how bad things really are.
- I might as well quit on this one, it's just not working.
- I'll never be as successful as they are.

Lets face it, it doesn't take much to be positive about yourself and the world around you when the sun is shining on you and your world is unfolding according to your own personal grand plan. It does however take effort and determination to maintain your positive mind-set when the sky above you is black and the world around you seems bent on making you the target for all that can go wrong. It's the times in your life when you have to create your own sunshine that you'll value your positive attitude the most. It's then the value of positive thinking is appreciated and its impact on the actions you take will be most beneficial.

Chapter Nineteen
What You See Is Who You Are

People interpret your thoughts through your actions.

It's been said that a little bit of knowledge can be a dangerous thing. On the other hand, a lot of thinking can also be a dangerous thing. Unless what you're thinking about supports what you want to accomplish. You are in many ways a prisoner to your thoughts. That's because your moods are created by your thoughts. The constructive, or destructive, actions you take are usually preceded by thoughts. That's why it's so important that your thoughts help rather than hinder your search for success. The thoughts rattling around in your head have an enormous impact on the success you plan to enjoy.

Whatever frame of mind you are in right now is the result of what you are thinking as you read this book. If you are concentrating on the message in the book your thoughts should be positive and constructive. Those thoughts should put you in a good mood and positive frame of mind. Your mood should be one of optimistic enjoyment. On the other hand if you're just skimming through the pages not tuned into or focused on the message your thoughts might wander and you could be thinking about the day you've had. If it was a challenging day your thoughts are likely to be negative and your mood will reflect that negativity. You are likely to be in less than an upbeat mood.

At any given moment you feel the way you do because of the thoughts you're thinking. Whether you jump out of bed in the morning ready and willing to go out and slay the daily dragons, or stumble out hoping the dragons have taken the day off, depends on your mood. That mood doesn't just happen. I can guarantee you it is the result of thinking about the day that lies ahead. I can also guarantee that you will have a lot more upbeat and productive days just by simply putting a positive spin on whatever the day has in store for you. The whole idea is pretty simple. When you wake in the morning and your immediate thoughts are positive you always bring a positive mood to bear on the actions you're going to take. If on the other you wake up and begin filling your thoughts with worry, concern, and negativity you are almost certain to bring an anxious and negative mood to bear on your actions throughout the day.

Productive sales professionals know all about the impact of positive vs negative thoughts and actions better than most. They put themselves and their emotions on the line everyday. They spend their days talking to people who hold the power to accept or reject their thoughts, ideas, services and products. A professional salesperson might start his or her day in a positive mood looking forward to meeting with a customer and closing a sale they've been working on. Then for whatever reason something goes wrong, the sale doesn't close and the opportunity is missed. Anyone who's ever experience a situation like that will confirm that you are left with a feeling of loss and rejection. At a time like that it's very difficult to not suffer a letdown and it's hard to avoid shoveling negatives into our thoughts. This momentary negativity is not in and of itself dangerous or harmful. In fact most normal people are going to have to let off a little steam at that point. It does get harmful if you let your negative thoughts and the accompanying pessimistic mood fester and grow. When that happens it can result in increased prospecting or sales call anxiety. In extreme cases this can manifest itself in a feeling of why bother they're not going to buy from me anyway. A frame of mind not likely to generate a lot of selling success. The end result is fewer sales and less desire to sell. The only way to break out of a negative force field like that is to stop thinking about what might have been and refocus your thoughts on what can be.

I've always marveled at how crystal clear and focused my thoughts are when I'm in a positive mood and how distorted and muddy they become when I'm not. The more negative the thoughts and mood the more distorted becomes the truth of the moment. It's a vicious circle. Negative thoughts precede and contribute to self-defeating emotional turmoil and destructive negative actions. This in turn distorts whatever situation you find yourself in. Even the most positive among us can't always keep some negativity from occasionally creeping into our thoughts. That's why on those occasions when it does we can benefit by learning how to deal with the distortions in thinking that occur during those lapses into negativity. When we learn how to recognize and deal effectively with the main culprits and their effects on us we can at least minimize the fall-out.

I refer to the distortions in thinking most common to salespeople as "thoughts that go bump in the night". You need to be able to recognize and deal with them because if you don't they can scare the career right out of you. I've listed some examples and ways to try overcoming them.

Playing defense. This kind of distorted thinking leads you react to almost everyone who criticizes your work by lashing back and being defensive. The need to prove the correctness of your ideas and points of view becomes the overriding issue for you during any and all discussions. Your sole focus is on proving your infallibility. It should be pretty obvious what the downside to this way of distorted thinking would be during any customer first selling situation. Every productive sales presentation calls for you to be focused on and discussing the needs and interests of your customer. Going into a defensive posture when questioned about the usefulness of various aspects of your product or service only serves to shine the spotlight more squarely on your customer's doubts.

Exchanges of ideas and information during any sales presentation should not be about winning or losing or parrying for points. It can't be about proving how right you are and how wrong they are. It needs to be about offering insights, expertise, information and opinions, with the understanding that both party's points of view carry equal weight. One way to keep yourself on the right track and avoid playing defense is to remind yourself that other people's opinions need to be shown the same respect that you feel yours deserve. Another way to overcome defensive distortion is by making a genuine effort to listen with an open mind to the reasoning behind other differing points of view, and make a genuine effort to find a middle ground.

Who's to blame here? This kind of distorted thinking leads to an all-consuming hunt to find some scapegoat you can make responsible for any negative results generated by your self-destructive feelings. If left unchecked this kind of distorted thinking develops into a siege mentality. It's always circumstances of someone else's making that force you to feel the way you do. You are never the author of your own misfortune. You need to understand and accept the notion that being a successful sales professional means you are directly responsible for your success or failure. In order for any of us to lead productive lives we first must accept responsibility and claim ownership for the results generated by how we think and act. The old adage; 'if it is to be, it is up to me' applies nicely here. We all have control right or wrong, good or bad, positive or negative over how we react to challenges and opportunities. It is a waste of your personal resources in terms of time, effort and energy to play the blame game. There is nothing positive to be gained by beating up on yourself or others because of failed efforts or momentary setbacks. Lessen the likelihood of who's to blame distortions by getting away from poor me thinking. When your efforts don't yield the expected results look first to the person behind the effort.

Gimme it all or don't gimme any. This kind of distorted thinking is often referred to as polarization. It causes you to think in extremes. To your way of thinking it's one hundred percent right or it's one hundred percent wrong. When you think this way your world becomes distorted through over-simplification. Everything in it is either black or white without any shades of gray. When we know in fact that the world around us is almost never that simple. This kind of thinking leads you to deal exclusively in all or nothing scenarios. Your attitude and outlook are influenced and controlled by a win it all and win at all costs mentality. Winning at all costs may be an admirable trait for a professional athlete. It isn't very productive for sales professionals who are concerned with the well being of their customers and it won't generate much in the way of repeat or referral business. Falling into the all or nothing trap doesn't leave you much room for error. With this type of thinking you don't cut yourself much slack. There is no room for you to settle for anything other than complete victory. The danger in this type of distorted thinking is that you end up putting your need for winning ahead of the interests of your customers. Your intent is to make the sale for the sake of making the sale. It doesn't matter whether or not it will benefit your customer. You may generate some short-term success with this mind-set but in the long term you'll find it impossible to maintain your credibility or produce repeat or referral business. There are lots of situations where you can't have all the pie, learn to appreciate the piece you get. To help overcome gimme it all distorted thinking learn to compromise. It might mean being the secondary supplier to some of your customers until your credibility grows and their trust in you earns you the number one spot.

Look into my crystal ball. This distorted thinking is the type most detrimental to sales professionals. Thinking this way convinces you that you have a unique ability to look into the future. You start to imagine the reaction customers are going to have to your product or service, well in advance of making your presentation. This type of thinking is actually the opposite end of the scale from positive visualization. What you see in your crystal ball is invariably negative. This kind of thinking results in a 'why make the effort' attitude with the accompanying lack of actions. When you can only see failure you can rest assured you will fail. I think you'll agree this is not the most productive mindset for sales professionals to have. The whole thought process begins with self destructive thoughts like 'they'll never do business with me' or 'they'll never pay what I charge when they can get it cheaper from somebody else' and inevitably builds into self-destructive behavior like 'why bother calling them at all'. Overcome this kind of distorted thinking by concentrating on the facts. Take into account only what you know for certain about the situation or circumstances you're dealing with, not what you image they might be. Be objective in your thoughts and put your subjective feelings aside. Stop thinking so much about what might happen and get active and see what does happen.

Umpiring. This type of distorted thinking causes you to begin to believe that you are the only one that knows what's fair and what isn't. Worse, you become resentful when others disagree with you. When you lose a sale it must be because the customer wasn't dealing fairly with you. You lost because they must have stacked the buying process in favor of their current supplier or no doubt the sales person for XYZ company is their distant cousin. Wake up and smell the coffee, in case you haven't heard let me be the one to tell you this startling piece of news, life isn't fair. Never has been, never will be. Wailing and moaning about fair or unfair is a waste of your time and emotional effort. If you go through life expecting every situation to be resolved using the rules and regulations of what is fair as laid down by you, you're just setting yourself up for disappointment. The real danger with this type of thinking is that disappointment can soon change to resentment and even hostility toward those you think are not playing fair according to your rules. Overcome this type of distorted thinking by reminding yourself when things don't go your way that the customer decides what's fair and sets the rules. Your choice is to decide whether or not to play.